The Way of the Mystics

Ancient Wisdom for Experiencing God Today

John Michael Talbot

with Steve Rabey

JOSSEY-BASS
A Wiley Company
San Francisco

Library of Congress Cataloging-in-Publication Data

Talbot, John Michael.
  The way of the mystics: ancient wisdom for experiencing God today/John Michael Talbot with Steve Rabey.
    p. cm.
  Includes bibliographical references.
  ISBN 0-7879-7572-9 (alk. paper)
  1. Mysticism—Catholic Church—History. 2. Spirituality—Catholic Church—History.
I. Rabey, Steve. II. Title.
  BV5082.3.T35 2005
  248.2'2—dc22   2004018419

Printed in the United States of America
FIRST EDITION
HB Printing   10 9 8 7 6 5 4 3 2 1

Contents

I dedicate this book to my personal spiritual father,
Fr. Martin Wolter, OFM, and to the founding bishop of the
Brothers and Sisters of Charity, Bishop Andrew McDonald,
Bishop Emeritus of Little Rock, Arkansas.

J.M.T.

I would like to thank agents Chip MacGregor and Steve Laube,
editors Julianna Gustafson and Joanne Clapp Fullagar
for devoted and tender editorial care, and the teachers at Denver
Seminary who inadvertently deepened my love for these mystics.

S.R.

Introduction

A Journey to the Heart of Our Faith

If you were to thoroughly examine your own spiritual life, what would you find?

Are you living a life of depth and reality, or do you sometimes feel that yours is a superficial existence that never seems to go beyond the senses, the emotions, and the intellect? Is God a living and breathing reality in the core of your being or merely a cold theological abstraction? Are you experiencing the fullness of Christ, or are you merely snacking on "Christianity lite"? And is your faith rooted and grounded in historic expressions of devotion that have stood the test of time, or is your spiritual experience confined to the most recent ecclesiastical trends and theories?

If you've ever asked yourself questions like these and not been entirely pleased with your answers, we would like to introduce you to some men and women who can show you a better way to live. These celebrated spiritual pioneers from some of the major Christian traditions devoted themselves to delving deeper into the reality of God. Thanks to them we have trusted guides along the spiritual journey who can usher us into the very heart of our faith.

From Words to Reality

Books like this one contain many words, ideas, and theological concepts. And although the rational discussion of religion is good and potentially very helpful, most of us would acknowledge that rationality is not the source of religion. Before it expresses itself in words and ideas, religion is born in experience.

"Mysticism is where religions start," writes author and pastor Frederick Buechner.

> Moses with his flocks in Midian, Buddha under the Bo tree, Jesus up to his knees in the waters of Jordan, each of them is responding to Something of which words like Shalom, Oneness, God even, are only pallid souvenirs. Religions start, as Frost said poems do, with a lump in the throat.

Most of us can describe certain aspects of our faith in words. If we couldn't do so, we would be locked up in our own private worlds, unable to connect with anyone else or compare notes about our varied journeys. The pages that follow contain many thousands of words, but as artists, physicists, and even linguists know all too well, words are humble devices that only poorly describe the deeper realities of our world and our souls.

If you do an Internet search on the word *mysticism*, you will see what a convoluted topic it is. Some people associate mysticism with all manner of emotional or spiritual excesses. Others confuse mysticism with heretical revelations, bizarre cults, messianic complexes, or even the auditory hallucinations associated with schizophrenia. Unfortunately, there is no shortage of historical figures to confuse the issues. For example, Rasputin was a devious man who used quasi-mystical mumbo jumbo to manipulate a Russian czar in the years before World War I.

The mystics in this book certainly had their share of otherworldly experiences, but their lives consisted of much more than a succession of odd occurrences. And although some of their contemporaries were convinced that these people had lost their senses, calmer voices have prevailed. In selecting the people we wanted to profile in these pages, my coauthor and I have steered clear of the more controversial and polarizing mystics of the past, focusing instead on those exceptional men and women who have been officially recognized as saints by the Catholic Church or have been embraced as exemplars of the faith by their own Protestant, Anglican, and Orthodox traditions.

Each of their stories is unique, but one common theme makes them especially interesting and worthy of our attention: they were divinely blessed to transcend the limitations that seem to close most of us off from the spiritual realm. This blessing enabled them to partake in the kind of communion that God desires to share with all of us.

In that sense, these thirteen mystics from different centuries, different countries, and different Christian traditions were truly pioneers of the spirit. Like the sailors who crossed the seas during the great age of discovery or the astronauts who now soar through the heavens, these spiritual pioneers temporarily transcended the bonds of earthly attachment to touch the face of God and taste the bliss of heaven. If you are a Christian, these pioneers are a part of your spiritual legacy. And even though they may have lived centuries ago, there is much you can learn from their lives that will help you today.

From Mind to Spirit

Scholars and theologians have debated the meaning of the term *mystic* for so long that some believe the word is impossible to define with any exactness. Perhaps it's appropriate that some of humanity's deepest and most ineffable spiritual longings can't be nailed down with clinical precision.

The working definition I use is a simple one that is directly connected to the concept of mystery, with which it shares a common Latin root word; the same root word appears in *sacrament*. But in short, a mystic is an ordinary person blessed by an extraordinary experience of God that transforms life in amazing ways. A mystic is someone who believes there are realities to life that are beyond what can be perceived by our rational minds or described in words. Further, a mystic not only believes this in the abstract but also desires to practice it in the concrete, allowing these deeper realities to permeate his or her life.

In a sense, every Christian who has a living, vital, and spirit-filled relationship with God can be considered a mystic. The goal of this book is to help you be a better mystic by learning from the wisdom of those who have gone before you.

Over the centuries, many Christian teachers (including some featured in this book) have employed the metaphor of marriage to help describe mysticism. Jesus referred to himself as a heavenly bridegroom who came to earth to receive his earthly bride. Similar bride-bridegroom themes appear in the writings of Jewish prophets like Isaiah, in John's depiction of heaven found in the book of Revelation, and in the writings of many other mystics down through the ages.

Having been married to a wonderful woman (and possibly a living saint!) named Viola for more than a decade, I can see how the marriage metaphor helps makes sense of the mystic's relationship with God. On the one hand, there is much about my relationship with Viola that is objective and easily described. We were married on a specific day in a specific place. We now live in a hermitage among members of our specific community in northwest Arkansas. Each one of us is of a specific age and has a particular height and weight.

On the other hand, there is much about our relationship that is mysterious and indescribable. There are thoughts and emotions we share that elude detection by any other human being and defy easy explanation. This "oneness" operates most powerfully on the level of intuition, which incorporates our senses, our emotions, and our thoughts but goes beyond them all while enriching them all. We share a closeness that enables us to anticipate each other's moods and attitudes, responses and reactions. After years of constant contact and communication, there is a soul connection between us that transcends mind and body.

Likewise, there are aspects of our relationship to God that cannot be scientifically analyzed or rationally explained. There's an essence to all of us that only God can awaken and touch. For many of us, this inner spiritual essence has been asleep for most of our lives, or it has been obscured by the cares of life or the ego, or it has been neglected due to our pursuit of possessions or sensations or the other demands in life.

When God connects with us essence-to-essence, spirit-to-spirit, this deepest part of us is awakened and energized, enabling us to experience a union with God that is both real and transcendent, both powerful and mysterious. This is the core of the mystical experience.

In the Christian tradition, sacraments like Holy Communion or the Eucharist or the Lord's Supper provide a public means for believers to share in such mysteries. Spiritual disciplines like prayer and meditation provide a more private means for such connection. Such tools are available to all of us, but it seems that some of history's better-known mystics have known a communion with God that was somehow deeper or more powerful than it is for most of us.

My coauthor and I pray that, through writing this book and studying the lives and words of the mystics, we can learn better how to experience such communion in our own lives. But in fairness, we should say that there's no such thing as a foolproof, step-by-step manual to the mystical life. If there were, spirituality wouldn't be a mystery! No one can predict when or where the wind of God's Holy Spirit will blow. The most we can hope for is to learn how to trim our sails so they can catch the wind when it does blow our way.

Mysticism is often called a religion of the heart, but we should never focus so much on our heart that we neglect the intellect. As we will see, some mystics talk about a movement from "knowing" to something they call "unknowing." But as advertisements for the United Negro College Fund once said, "A mind is a terrible thing to waste." My relationship with Viola involves body, mind, and spirit working together in tandem. Likewise, our relationship with God should involve all the aspects of our being.

The mystics featured in this book model a healthy balance among all of these faculties, and their wisdom can help us avoid the many excesses and extremes that have bedeviled so many over the past twenty centuries.

A Mystical Faith

There are mystics in all religions. Even people who have no religious affiliation or any belief in God may have mystic-like experiences through their contact with the beauties of nature or the power of great works of music, literature, or art. There are also ancient shamanic traditions that seek contact with otherworldly powers through trances or psychoactive drugs. Some thinkers in the fast-growing field of neurotheology have even described humans as mystical animals who are hard-wired for transcendental experience. And there's no disputing the fact that techniques like meditation yield measurable physiological benefits that help Christians and Buddhists alike.

Our focus in this book will be on the mystic heart of the Christian faith, which was seen most clearly in the life of Christ, who told the woman at the well: "God is spirit, and his worshipers must worship in spirit and truth" (John 4:24). Jesus experienced a unique form of union with his Heavenly Father. And although we can't duplicate his intimacy with God, we can follow his example in our efforts to grow closer to God.

The truth of Jesus' words was demonstrated with power on the Day of Pentecost, when the Holy Spirit filled believers in ways no one had ever seen before. Not all Christians realize it, but ever since that Day of Pentecost, Christianity has continued to be a deeply mystical and spiritually charged faith.

Today, many people equate Christianity with religious legalism, political activism, or bureaucratic institutionalism, but they are missing the heart of the story. The church of Jesus Christ has an important and ancient tradition of contemplative spirituality, and mystics have founded major movements and monasteries, written influential books about theology and the inner life, and served as role models for millions of believers looking for reliable spiritual guides.

Historically, mysticism has been strongest in the Roman Catholic and Eastern Orthodox traditions, but mystics have also flourished in Protestant and Anglican traditions, and we will meet some of them as well.

The theological thread that weaves all these stories of faith together can be found in three foundations of Christian mysticism:

1. God exists.

2. God is personal.

3. God desires a personal communion with each and every one of us.

These foundations represent the *knowable* aspects of God and are part of his *emanation* into all creation. But there are some aspects of God that transcend all human grasping. God is beyond all such descriptions and classifications of image, name, or form. Here, even the charismatic experiences of the gifts of the Spirit, visions and revelations, are but stages we pass through on our journey to the pure mystical experience of passive contemplation.

Mystical experiences are not intended to replace sound theology. Rather, they are the experiential outgrowth of sound theology, infusing it with life and connecting to the very core of our being. Such experiences are an important part of the mystical journey, but they will always remain a great mystery, and the words we use to describe them are feeble and imperfect.

Winds of Change

A man named Nicodemus once asked Jesus about eternal life. His answer was both simple and profound: "The wind blows wherever it pleases. You hear its sound, but you cannot tell where it comes from or where it is going. So it is with everyone born of the Spirit" (John 3:8).

As we saw earlier, the realm of the human and the divine—the human spirit and the Holy Spirit—is the real core of our being. Spirit is essence that is found in God and all creation and is found in the human being in such a special way that, throughout the history of Western theology, we have often been described as "created in the image of God" *(imago dei)*. The Buddhists call this place of essential being the "face before we are born." Others call it the "ground of being." Whatever it is called in various traditions, it is a fundamental aspect of human life and remains the core of the Being of God.

Jesus taught that we must die to our old way of living and be born again to a whole new way of being that enlivens every aspect of how we perceive and live life. Jesus calls this "abundant life."

Mystics have been around forever, but history suggests that the wind of the Spirit has blown more strongly during some periods of human history than others. I've witnessed this myself during the last few decades, as an intense hunger for all things spiritual has manifested itself in the growing worldwide popularity of charismatic worship, the so-called New Age movement, and the interest in books, tapes, and seminars on spiritual transformation. These signs, along with countless personal conversations, indicate that we may be living during one such period right now. And Bernard McGinn, one of the leading experts on mysticism, agrees. "The past two decades have witnessed a remarkable resurgence of interest in the study and practice of Christian spirituality," McGinn writes.

Interest in mysticism seems to increase during times of cultural and religious upheaval, including periods of religious renewal and reform. For example, St. Benedict and St. Francis were mystics who lived during times of intense social transformation, and the new models of spirituality that they gave to their followers helped reform the entire church.

But interest waned in other periods. The Enlightenment of the eighteenth century emphasized rationalism, scientific inquiry, and humanism, thus ushering in an attitude of skepticism concerning spiritual things. Negative attitudes toward mysticism have also been heightened during the past two centuries by a widespread condemnation of a seventeenth-century spiritual movement called

Quietism that emphasized human passivity and claimed people could achieve a sinless state. Critics accused Quietist leaders like Madame Guyon and Francois Fenelon of undervaluing the role of the intellect and downplaying the role of human responsibility in spiritual growth.

In the 1960s, the West went through a period of profound social and religious upheaval. Culturally, an international youth counterculture was being born and was expressing itself through new forms of music, new lifestyles, and increased social activism. Spiritually, movements like the charismatic movement and the Jesus movement injected new life into many churches, while Vatican II brought major reform to the Catholic Church.

The wind of the Spirit that was blowing during the 1960s helped bring me to faith in Christ. I was a young musician traveling with the folk-rock band, Mason Proffitt, and our long hours on the road gave me plenty of time to indulge my deep spiritual hunger by studying books on Buddhism, Hinduism, and Native American spirituality. Ultimately, it was a mystical apparition of Jesus in my room at a Holiday Inn in 1971 that led to my becoming a Christian. Perhaps God used such means to reach me because I was too dull to get the message any other way.

I hope this book may be of help to people who want to learn from the Christian spiritual masters but don't have the time, the patience, or the theological training to wade through dozens of dusty volumes. My coauthor and I have done the legwork for you and have provided here an introduction to the lives, the teachings, and the lessons to be learned from some of the faith's most trusted guides. We come from different branches of the Christian family, but this makes our collaboration on writing projects, which began in 1997 with *The Lessons of St. Francis*, even stronger. I am a Catholic who has devoted the last two decades of my life to exploring the relevance of the monastic and Franciscan traditions in our own day. Steve is a Protestant whose pilgrimage has led him to a deeper appreciation of some of the faith's more ancient practices. Together, we hope to provide an introduction to the mystical way that transcends petty differences and provides encouragement and direction to anyone who wants to know Christ more deeply.

The mystics of the past were not spiritual superstars or privileged members of some esoteric elite. They were people like you and me. It is our hope that as you read the pages that follow, the time-tested attitudes and disciplines they developed over the centuries will help you raise your sails and better enable you to catch the wind of God's Spirit.

Knowing and Unknowing

We live in an age of information, but there is much about the mystical life that cannot be reduced to the common categories of human knowledge. In the ancient tradition of Christian mystical theology, there are things that are *cataphatic*, or knowable, and things that are *apophatic*, or unknowable.

The knowable things are apprehended by body, soul, or mind and involve our senses, emotions, and thoughts—doctrines regarding faith and morality, ascetic practices, and spiritual disciplines like meditation.

The unknowable things are in the realm of mysticism. These include ecstatic and rapturous charismatic union, experiences of peace and rest, and fruits of passive contemplation. These essences are apprehended by the direct intuition of the spirit.

God is Spirit, and when he created humanity he desired that Spirit would be the foundation of our lives. But in this fallen world, most of us have turned this priority upside down, and the body and soul usually come first.

There's a spiritual essence to all of us that only God can awaken and touch. For many of us, this inner essence has been asleep for most of our lives, or it has been obscured by the cares of life or the ego, or it has been neglected due to our pursuit of possessions or sensations or other demands in life. By learning the wisdom of the mystics, we can learn how to make things right again, giving our spiritual essence the priority it deserves.

LEARNING MORE ABOUT
Mysticism

Many books are available on all kinds of mysticism. Two of the best and most accessible books about Christian mysticism were written by twentieth-century Anglican writer Evelyn Underhill, who devoted much of her life to understanding and interpreting this amazingly vast topic. By the time of her death in 1941, she had written more than three dozen books about the life of the spirit, but her classic is *Mysticism* (1911, various publishers). Equally valuable is her 1925 study, *Mystics of the Church* (1925, Morehouse).

A more thorough examination can be found in Bernard McGinn's impressive four-volume series, *The Presence of God: A History of Western Christian Mysticism* (Crossroad, 1990s). McGinn, a professor in the Divinity School of the University of Chicago, covers an amazingly broad territory without losing his readers in the process. Additional recommendations are found at the conclusion of each of the chapters.

A note on where to find books: though authors dream of writing books that will be around as long as Athanasius's *Life of Antony*, publishers face many practical concerns that mean many of the books we are recommending may be out of print. Therefore, let us recommend the Web site abebooks.com, which lets you shop for titles by scanning the inventory of thousands of used bookstores around the world. And information on my own books and recordings can be found at johnmichaeltalbot.com.

The Way of the Desert
Antony and the Desert Fathers

When a sensitive, searching soul named Antony experienced a powerful revelation of God around the year 270, the reverberations not only transformed his life but permanently altered the way Christians throughout the world put their faith into practice.

The biographer Athanasius says Antony was born to "parents of good birth and good means." They were also devout, and Antony often accompanied them to church. But after they died, eighteen-year-old Antony was left to ponder his fate.

One day as he walked to church, Antony found himself thinking about the radical devotion of the earliest Christians. Hadn't Peter and other disciples forsaken everything to follow their master? And hadn't the believers featured in the book of Acts shared all their earthly goods with anyone who had need?

Once he got to church, Antony heard a reading from Chapter Nineteen of the gospel of Matthew. After blessing a group of children, Jesus is approached by a man who asks him this point-blank question: "Teacher, what good thing must I do to get eternal life?"

Jesus seldom gave direct answers to such questions. In this case, he talked with the man about the many commandments in the Hebrew Scriptures.

"All these I have kept," said the man. "What do I still lack?"

Jesus looked him in the eyes and replied: "If you want to be perfect, go, sell your possessions and give to the poor, and you will have treasure in heaven."

Nearly twenty centuries later, we can still read the man's pain between the lines of Matthew's narrative. "When the young man heard this, he went away sad, because he had great wealth."

But for Antony, the reading turned on a light in his troubled soul. It was like God had tapped him on the shoulder and commanded him to turn his back on his life of prosperity and privilege. "As soon as he went out of the church he gave to the villagers the property he had from his parents," writes Athanasius.

This was dry and dusty Egypt, where fertile land was as good as gold. But after giving away three hundred acres of prime property that had been in his family for generations, Antony sold his remaining personal goods, giving most of the money to the poor and only "keeping a little because of his sister."

On another Sunday morning, Antony heard a reading from the Sermon on the Mount. Jesus was concluding his moving sermon on God's loving care for the birds of the air and the lilies of the field. "Therefore do not worry about tomorrow, for tomorrow will worry about itself." These words stirred Antony to give away even the paltry amount he had held back.

"He could not bear to wait longer," writes Athanasius, "but went out and distributed this also to the poor." Next he entrusted his sister to a group of Christian women and began living a life of solitude and hardship on the outskirts of town.

The devil frequently tempted Antony with visions of material comfort, and passing townspeople often disturbed his solitude. But Antony resolved to devote himself to God more fully, demonstrating his faith with fasts, sleepless nights, long periods of kneeling and prayer, and other self-inflicted punishments. "Each day, as though then beginning his religious life, he made greater effort to advance."

He also moved further away from the hubbub of village life, asking a trusted friend to lock him into a nearby tomb where he endured long-running battles with demons who tried to wear him down with their deadliest sins: pride, envy, anger, sloth, lust, avarice, and gluttony. Just when it looked as though Antony might fall, Jesus appeared in a brilliant beam of light that pierced the tomb's murky darkness and made this astounding promise to his wearied but faithful servant: "Since thou has endured and not yielded, I will always be thy Helper, and I will make thee renowned everywhere."

Antony was now about thirty-five years old, and the next step on his spiritual pilgrimage was the most dramatic yet. He turned and walked away from his home town, leaving all behind and heading alone into Egypt's burning deserts, where he spent the remaining seven decades of his life surviving on crumbs of bread, sips of water, marathons of prayer, visions of heavenly paradise, and an abiding sense of God's comforting presence.

This solitary pilgrimage would become the model for other spiritual seekers who followed Antony's footsteps and, as one scholar said, such devotion to solitude "taught us how man makes himself eternal."

"There is nothing to consider," said Antony.

> If we do not forsake these things for virtue's sake, still we leave them later on when we die. Why not rather possess those things which we can take away with us—prudence, justice, temperance, fortitude, understanding, charity, love of the poor, gentleness, hospitality?

Blossoms in the Desert

For millennia, deserts have provided important arenas for God's dealings with humanity. After their exodus from slavery in Egypt, the people of Israel spent forty years wandering in deserts, seeking their promised land. The wild-eyed John the Baptist taught and baptized followers in the deserts of Judea. And after Jesus' own baptism by John, the Spirit of God led him into the desert, where he was tempted by the devil for forty days and nights before beginning his earthly ministry.

The Desert Fathers and Their Time

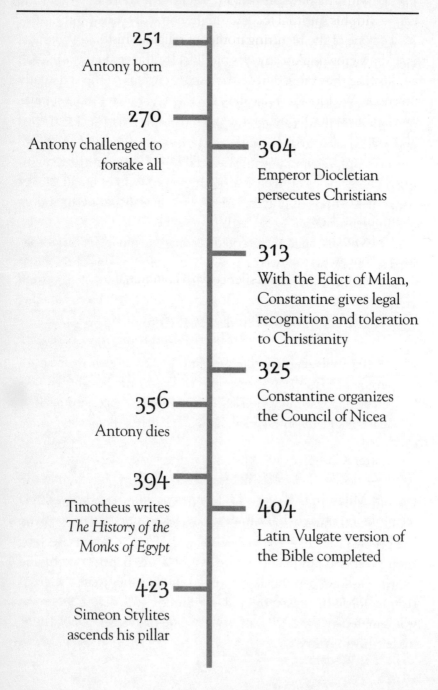

251

Antony born

270

Antony challenged to
forsake all

304

Emperor Diocletian
persecutes Christians

313

With the Edict of Milan,
Constantine gives legal
recognition and toleration
to Christianity

325

Constantine organizes
the Council of Nicea

356

Antony dies

394

Timotheus writes
*The History of the
Monks of Egypt*

404

Latin Vulgate version of
the Bible completed

423

Simeon Stylites
ascends his pillar

Antony (251–356) saw the desert as the site where one could wrestle with the devil in person, so he went there to engage the battle with his spiritual foe and single-handedly defeat him.

But one of the recurring ironies of religious history is that hermits draw crowds. Antony was no different; he gradually attracted a following that ranged from the mildly curious to the spiritually ravenous. Within a few decades, thousands of men (and a smaller number of women) sought God in the dry, dusty deserts of the Middle East.

Antony's specialty was spiritual warfare, not pastoral oversight. That's where a man named Pachomius (290–347) came in. He founded an Egyptian monastery around 320 that brought together a handful of hermit monks into a community. The word *monk* comes from the Greek word *monos*, which means "one, alone," hence, "one who lives alone." Pachomius's approach balanced adequate time for solitude and silence with communal living in houses of ten members under the supervision of a superior. The monks also gathered daily for common worship and work.

By the time of his death, he oversaw some nine thousand monks and nuns in numerous monasteries. In time, Pachomius's *cenobetical* (or communal) model would become more popular than Antony's *eremetical* (or solitary) approach, giving form to a Christian monastic movement that remains strong today.

What was once a trickle of hermits and monks turned into a flood after Constantine—the emperor of the Western Roman Empire—declared Christianity the official faith of the realm in the Edict of Milan in the year 313. Christians who had endured two centuries of official harassment and persecution were now to become a dominant force in the world's reigning superpower. Although most Christians welcomed the chance to own property, live in peace, and even play a role in civic affairs, others were horrified by Constantine's marriage of church and state, cross and crown.

Thomas Merton, the twentieth century's most famous monk (see the last chapter in this book) described this transition in his book, *The Wisdom of the Desert:*

Society . . . was regarded by them as a shipwreck from which each single individual man had to swim for his life. . . . The fact that the Emperor was now Christian and that the "world" was coming to know the Cross as a sign of temporal power only strengthened them in their resolve.

Soon communities of prayer were blooming in those deserts located along the Nile and surrounding Jerusalem. As Athanasius tells us, "The monasteries in the hills were like tents filled with heavenly choirs." And although the vast majority of these hermits and monks died as they had lived—unknown and unheralded— those who were leaders of communities and who left behind a record of their teaching would become known as the Desert Fathers and Mothers.

Pilgrims and Penitents

St. Jerome was a scholar whose Vulgate translation of the Bible from Hebrew to Latin would be the Western world's primary translation for a millennium. But as a young man, Jerome prowled the deserts of the Middle East in search of saintly teachers. One of his favorites was Paul of Thebes—a man Jerome believed to be "the first hermit." Some people dismissed Paul as "a man in an underground cavern with hair to his heels," but Jerome admired his saintly devotion and hailed him as one who "lived the life of heaven upon earth."

Another chronicler of the Desert Christians was a monk named Cassian (365–435), who traveled throughout the Middle East visiting monasteries and recording the sayings of monks in his two classic books, *Institutes* and *Conferences*. A century later, these volumes would influence St. Benedict, whose famous Rule for monasteries (see the end of the next chapter for more description) remains influential today.

The accounts of the hermits and monks who flourished in the desert feature a colorful and eclectic group of religious eccentrics who paid little heed to social conventions. According to Athanasius, Antony "never bathed his body in water for cleanliness, nor even washed his feet, nor would he consent to put them in water at all without necessity." Abbot Arsenius kept a container of foul-smelling water in his humble hut. "For the incense and the fragrance of the perfumes that I used in the world, needs must I use this stench now." Abbot Agatho kept a stone in his mouth for three years until he learned the discipline of silence. And the hermit Theon reportedly kept silent for thirty years, occasionally extending his hand through the window of his hut to heal those who waited patiently outside.

Their individual spiritual disciplines and personal idiosyncrasies varied widely, but the one thing that united all those who fled to the desert was their conviction that practicing a pure and powerful brand of Christianity required getting away from the corrosive influences of sinful, secular society.

"Unless a man shall say in his heart, 'I alone and God are in this world,' he shall not find quiet," said Abbot Allois. Antony compared hermits to fish. "Fish, if they tarry on dry land, die," he said. "Even so monks that tarry outside their cell or abide with men of the world fall away from their vow of quiet. As fish must return to the sea, so must we to our cell." Or, as Abbot Marcus put it when a dear friend asked why he had to flee the fellowship of humanity: "God knows that I love you: but I cannot be with God and with men."

Marcus's comment shows that the monks' solitude wasn't merely an escape from the hustle and bustle of the outside world but an entry point to deeper communication with God. For most of us, daily life is full of so many distractions that we are never able to turn the noise down low enough to hear ourselves think, let alone spend time in silent conversation with God. These Desert Christians remind us how important it is to set aside time and space for God.

Thomas Merton praised the Desert Christians for their commitment to silence and solitude. "What the Fathers sought most of all was their own true self, in Christ," he wrote. "And in order to do this, they had to reject completely the false, formal self, fabricated under social compulsion in 'the world.' "

A desert monk named Abbot Pastor once taught about the many obstacles that interfere with prayer, even in a monastery. "If you cannot catch the wind, neither can you prevent distracting thoughts from coming into your head," he said. "Your job is to say No to them." For Abbot Pastor and many other men and women like him, the best way to say no to life's many distractions was to seek a place for prayer that was quiet and separated from the cacophony of the world.

Athletes of God

Some of those who first wrote about the Desert Fathers called them "the athletes of God." It's an apt description, considering that many of these early monks were as relentless in their self-discipline as athletes preparing for the Olympics or other Greco-Roman contests of skill and endurance.

The Apostle Paul compared the rigors of the Christian life to an athletic contest in his first letter to the Corinthians:

> Do you not know that in a race all the runners run, but only one gets the prize? Run in such a way as to get the prize. Everyone who competes in the games goes into strict training. They do it to get a crown that will not last; but we do it to get a crown that will last forever. Therefore I do not run like a man running aimlessly; I do not fight like a man beating the air. No, I beat my body and make it my slave so that after I have preached to others, I myself will not be disqualified for the prize.

In her acclaimed and accessible 1936 book, *The Desert Fathers*, Helen Waddell argues that the self-inflicted exertions of the early monks and hermits showed the depth of their belief that "passion must be dug out by the roots."

Skimping on food was one way to get at the roots of desire, and the Desert Christians were masters at fasting. One Desert Father recommended a moderate approach: "I would have it so that every day one should deny one's self a little in eating, so as not to be satisfied." But others adopted a more rigorous regimen. One elderly monk told a younger man how he conquered the desires of the flesh: "Since the time that I became a monk I have never given myself my fill of bread, nor of water, nor of sleep, and tormenting myself with appetite for these things whereby we are fed, I was not suffered to feel the stings of lust." Another old monk confessed, "Indeed, brother, I had forgotten what solace men may have in food."

Although some of the Desert Christians competed to eat less than their brethren, others engaged in contests of virtue. *The History of the Monks of Egypt* was written around 394 by a traveling monk named Timotheus. He observed that the monks were "quiet and gentle" until it came to demonstrating their superior godliness. "They have indeed a great rivalry among them," he wrote. "It is who shall be more merciful than his brother, kinder, humbler, and more patient."

Timotheus's *History* includes the following memorable anecdote:

> They tell that once a certain brother brought a bunch of grapes to the holy Macarius: but he who for love's sake thought not on his own things but on the things of others, carried it to another brother, who seemed more feeble. And the sick man gave thanks to God for the kindness of his brother, but he too thinking more of his neighbor than himself, brought it to another, and he again to another, and so that same bunch of grapes was carried round all the cells, scattered as they were far over the desert, and no one knowing who first had sent it, it was brought at last to the first giver.

Timotheus never reveals whether or not Macarius actually ate the grapes. Perhaps too many monkish hands had turned them to mush by the time they arrived back at his hut. But Timotheus does inform us that the whole episode inspired the dedicated monk to even greater spiritual rigors. "The holy Macarius gave thanks that he had seen in the brethren such abstinence and such loving-kindness and did himself reach after still sterner discipline of the life of the spirit."

Assessing Antony's Legacy

Before he died at the ripe old age of 104, Antony told his disciples to bury him in an unmarked grave so that none would turn his bones into holy relics. But no amount of graveside secrecy would diminish Antony's lasting and complex legacy.

One thing is clear: Antony and his disciples preached a demanding, all-or-nothing brand of Christianity that required wholehearted commitment. One story tells how Antony dealt with a brother who wanted to renounce the world but still cling to a few prized possessions:

> When the elder heard about all this, he said to him: If you want to be a monk, go to that village and buy meat, and place it on your naked body and return here. And when the brother had done as he was told, dogs and birds of prey tore at his body. Then Abbot Antony said: Those who renounce the world and want to retain possession of money are assailed and torn apart by devils just as you are.

This may have been an extreme form of Christianity, but it challenges all of us to do more than merely join a church, attend services, and drop checks into the offering basket. Jesus walked the earth, issuing this invitation to men and women: "Follow me." Then as now, accepting this invitation should cost us something.

The Desert Christians also served as a bridge between the East, with its emphasis on mystery and experience, and the West, with its emphasis on rationality and doctrine. "In many respects, these Desert Fathers had much in common with Indian yogis and with Zen Buddhist monks of China and Japan," wrote Thomas Merton (see the last chapter of this book), who spent much of his life studying the devotional practices of Eastern faiths. I believe this bridge between East and West is even more important in our present age of religious diversity than it was in Antony's day.

I also appreciate the Desert Christians' radical countercultural stance. The Emperor Constantine worked overtime to harness the energy of the church to the ambitions of the state, but the hermits and monks stood against the seductive allure of worldly power and prestige. Today, debates about church and state stir up deep feelings around the globe. What better time to insist, with the Desert Fathers, that the church is ultimately a mystical entity, not the religious branch of secular culture.

Some aspects of desert spirituality seem out of balance, such as the wholesale dismissal of the physical aspects of God's creation, including the human body. It's one thing for us to discipline our bodily desires, which would control our lives if we didn't rein them in. It's another thing to state, as Abbot Daniel did, that the body is the enemy of the soul. "Even as the body flourisheth, so doth the soul become withered," said Daniel, "and when the body is withered, then doth the soul put forth leaves." Or as another Desert Christian named Dorotheus the Theban put it, "I kill my body, for it kills me."

This incomplete theology led some Desert Fathers to equate self-inflicted physical tortures with spiritual maturity. They also mistakenly assumed that women were the cause of sexual lust, which led many communities to exclude women members. (An exception was made for an abbess named Sara, who was "a woman in sex, but not in spirit"!) Jesus certainly advocated moral purity, but he never turned his back on women. And although Jesus rigorously prayed and fasted, he didn't make himself gaunt and emaciated the way many of the most esteemed Desert Fathers did.

Many Desert Christians also undervalued the importance of the mind. Once a young brother approached Abbot Moses and asked him for guidance. Moses told the young man, "Go, sit in your cell, and your cell will teach you everything." And Antony once told a group of disciples that books were an unnecessary luxury. "To one whose mind is sound, letters are needless," he said. We all can think of people who are puffed up or intellectually arrogant. And many of us know more in our heads than we practice in our lives. But that doesn't mean the mind shouldn't play an important role in our spiritual lives. (We will see in later chapters that many mystics failed to embrace a balanced approach to the mind.)

Perhaps one of the biggest problems with Antony's movement was its insistence that true faith required a near-total separation from the world. As H. Richard Niebuhr points out in his classic volume *Christ and Culture*, the "debate about relations of Christianity and civilization" represents the "enduring problem" of Christian faith. The rise of fundamentalism in our own lifetime is further evidence of this ongoing debate about how best to relate to the wider world.

Some historians have been particularly harsh in their condemnation of the Desert Christians. Edward Gibbon, the famous eighteenth-century historian, called them "horrid and disgusting." He wrote in *Decline and Fall of the Roman Empire*:

> A hideous, distorted and emaciated maniac, without knowledge, without patriotism, without natural affection, spending his life in a long routine of useless and atrocious self-torture, and quailing before the ghastly phantoms of his delirious brain, had become the ideal of the nations which had known the writings of Plato and Cicero and the lives of Socrates and Cato. . . . They were sunk under the painful weight of crosses and chains; and their emaciated limbs were confined by collars, bracelets, gauntlets, and greaves of massy and rigid iron. . . . Some savage saints of both sexes have been admired, whose naked bodies were only covered by their long hair.

Some of the hermits living in Egypt and Syria in the centuries after Antony even turned their deprivations into circus sideshows. Around the year 423, a monk named Simeon Stylites decided he would demonstrate his devotion to God by climbing up a tall pillar and never coming down. At the time of his death more than thirty years later, his final pillar stood fifty-five feet above the desert floor. Over the next five centuries, hundreds of "stylites" would follow this dubious example, demonstrating that religious extremism is a very old tradition.

Nobody is perfect, and I pray that any future writers who examine my spiritual life are merciful about my many errors. Still, it's by carefully evaluating the practices of the past that we can best determine what we should incorporate into our own spiritual lives.

Heeding the Call of the Desert

No one would mistake the emerald-green glens of Ireland for the barren deserts of the Middle East, but the Celtic monks who lived in the centuries after St. Patrick patterned their lives after the Desert Christians and created monasteries in outposts like Dysert O'Dea in County Clare, Dysert in County Limerick, and Dysart and Dysart Tola in County Westmeath. Even though their humble monasteries were battered by Atlantic gales and drenched by spring rains, these wet Irish monks set their hearts on the spiritual disciplines of the desert.

We can do the same thing in our own lives, and we don't need a desert to follow the principles of desert spirituality. One thing Antony teaches is that you must start your quest with yourself. So many of us follow the crowd or casually trust our spiritual growth to the care of others. Others among us are so wrapped up in compulsive, codependent, or destructive relationships that a million painful bonds tether our hearts. But you can begin heeding the call of the desert by spending time alone with God in silence and solitude.

Experiencing silence and solitude may take some work in the midst of our noisy and chaotic culture. Perhaps you can begin by scheduling periodic fasts from pop culture and mass media entertainment. You may also want to schedule regular outdoor walks or hikes. Weekend retreats at monasteries or spiritual centers are another way to intentionally focus your energies on God (see the chapter entitled "The Way of the Pilgrim").

Renunciation is a key concept of desert spirituality. Antony and his disciples renounced many things: the devil, the allure of worldly pleasures, basic bodily appetites for food and sleep, and the enticements of the seven deadly sins (pride, envy, anger, sloth, lust, avarice, and gluttony). Is there anything in your life you need to renounce? What has a hold on your soul?

In 1994, I released a recording titled *Meditations from Solitude*. Two of the songs on that album are based on the writings of Evagrios of Pontus, a mystic and theologian who lived part of his life in the desert and wrote about the deadly sins. One of these songs is called "Renounce All," and the chorus says:

> *Renounce all to gain everything*
> *You will then be free of all things.*

The other song is titled "The Desert/Separated from All." The opening verse says:

> *Blessed the soul, the soul alone*
> *Undisturbed at times of prayer*
> *Blessed the soul free of every possession*
> *Blessed the soul, the soul alone.*

Perhaps these simple verses can serve as an invitation to you to heed the call of the desert. Perhaps you juggle a busy workload with responsibilities to family and other duties. You may even live in Antarctica. But God still calls you to the desert of the heart where he invites you to commune with him alone.

Sayings of the Desert Fathers

Thousands of desert hermits and monks—we have no record of most of them—lived and died anonymously. But the teachings of some of the leading desert abbots were gathered together in *Sayings of the Elders* and other ancient collections. These sayings, some of which resemble Buddhist koans (paradoxes to be meditated upon), are so powerful and pithy that they cross the centuries to speak to us today. (The sayings that follow are anonymous unless otherwise indicated.)

One of the Fathers said: Just as it is impossible for a man to see his face in troubled water, so too the soul, unless it be cleansed of alien thoughts, cannot pray to God in contemplation.

Unless thou first amend thy life going to and fro amongst men, thou shall not avail to amend it dwelling alone. (Abbot Lucius)

Teach your heart to keep what your tongue teaches others. (Abbot Poemen)

The man that every hour hath death before his eyes, will conquer meanness of soul.

Even as wax is melted before the face of fire, so is the soul enfeebled by praise, and loses the toughness of its virtues. (the holy Syncletica)

If [the] brother who carries his fast for six days were to hang himself up by the nostrils, he could not equal the other, who does service to the sick.

There is no need of much speaking in prayer, but often stretch out thy hands and say, "Lord, as Thou wilt and as Thou knowest, have mercy upon me." And because He knoweth what we have need of, He showeth us His mercy. (Abbot Macarius)

The prayer of the monk is not perfect until he no longer realizes himself or the fact that he is praying. (Antony of the Desert)

LEARNING MORE ABOUT
Antony and the Desert Fathers

The best source for understanding the Desert Fathers remains Athanasius's *Life of St. Antony*. Even though it was written more than sixteen centuries ago, the book remains accessible to modern readers and is available in numerous editions. We prefer the edition that is part of the impressive Paulist Press series, The Classics of Western Spirituality (see www.paulistpress.org). We will refer to this series many times before this book is done.

John Cassian's *Conferences* can also be found in this series or on the Internet site "The Christian Classics Ethereal Library" (www.ccel.org).

There are a number of more recent books written about desert spirituality, and we find Thomas Merton's brief *The Wisdom of the Desert* (New Directions, 1960) particularly worthwhile. Other excellent studies include Helen Waddell's *The Desert Fathers* (The University of Michigan Press, 1957, 1936), Benedicta Ward's *The Lives of the Desert Fathers* (Cistercian, 1980), Jacque Lacarriere's *Men Possessed by God* (Doubleday, 1964), and Belden C. Lane's *The Solace of Fierce Landscapes: Exploring Desert and Mountain Spirituality* (Oxford, 1998).

Christian History magazine devoted an entire issue to exploring "St. Antony & the Desert Fathers: Extreme Faith in the Early Church" (issue 64, www.christianhistory.net), and this volume remains an excellent brief summary of a complex movement.

For more on hermits, see Isabel Colgate's *A Pelican in the Wilderness: Hermits, Solitaires and Recluses* (Counterpoint, 2002), and for a contemporary look at desert spirituality, see William Dalrymple's excellent *From the Holy Mountain: A Journey Among the Christians of the Middle East* (Holt, 1997).

Some of my observations on present-day monastic and contemplative spirituality can be found in my book, *Hermitage*. An account of my own hermitage in the Indiana woods can be found in "Holy Man in the Woods"—a chapter in Dan O'Neill's biography, *Signatures: The Story of John Michael Talbot*. And songs about desert and contemplative spirituality can be found in my album, *Meditations from Solitude*.

The Way of Love
Bernard of Clairvaux

We've all heard preachers who'd rather lace their words with vinegar than with honey. If pressured, they would say their mission is proclaiming the Good News of Jesus, but they sure make that good news sound awfully depressing and condemning.

These prophets of doom love sermons patterned after Jonathan Edwards's Great Awakening classic, *Sinners in the Hands of an Angry God*. And they would rather scare people into heaven by describing the horrors of hell or the chaos of the earth's wretched final days than tickle people's ears with hopeful homilies about God's love and grace.

This was not the way of Bernard of Clairvaux—one of the most beloved and influential religious leaders of the Middle Ages, who earned the nickname "doctor mellifluous" because he preferred the sweet over the bitter. "Jesus is honey in the mouth, music in the ear and a shout of joy in the heart," wrote this warm, witty, and caring monk.

When the charismatic twenty-one-year-old Bernard entered the new French monastery of Citeaux, he persuaded nearly thirty close friends and relatives to join with him. When he preached at the University of Paris, his winsome words caused many conversions and persuaded numerous students to be ordained. And whenever he was scheduled to speak in towns and villages throughout his native France, fearful women reportedly hid their sons and sent their husbands out on chores.

The most famous of Bernard's many books was *On Loving God*. He also preached hundreds of sermons in which he described a

Heavenly Father who was so kind and loving that people felt compelled to love him back. And for Bernard, there was nothing better than experiencing an intimate relationship with God. "Its sweetness seizes the whole heart and draws it completely from the love of all flesh and every sensual pleasure," he wrote.

The way people understand the gospel has a lot to do with their notions about human nature and God. Vinegar-style preachers prey on people's fears because they believe people are basically sinful, rebellious, or stupid. Bernard was more optimistic; he wrote lengthy treatises about the dignity of human nature and believed that people would love God more deeply if preachers appealed to their loving natures.

And the God Bernard worshipped wasn't the kind to grab people around their necks and demand their attention but was a loving Heavenly Father who woos us with the surpassing fragrance of his love. "All his words contain supernatural mysteries and are full of heavenly sweetness, if only they have a diligent reader," wrote Bernard. "Put your ear to the door, strain to listen to the tidings he brings. Maybe you will hear soothing words to comfort you."

For Bernard, love was no abstract theological concept; it was the experiential reality of his daily life. A devout mystic who frequently found himself lost in heavenly raptures, he used his skills as a communicator to describe his spiritual experiences and encourage others to enjoy similar encounters. And in a series of sermons that was left uncompleted at his death, he explored the erotic imagery of the Old Testament's *Song of Songs*, finding in the book's earthy love poetry an image of God's passionate love for his children.

Bernard, who lived during the twelfth century, was a complex man who served as a counselor to popes, a founder of monasteries, a fighter against heresies and, to his lasting regret, a promoter of the disaster known as the Second Crusade. But today he is probably the best known and most beloved of the mystics in this book, and his good tidings of heavenly blessings still warm hearts as they did when he first preached them so long ago.

"It was as if a gentle southerly wind were blowing," he said. "It was as if the Sun of righteousness were shining close by, causing sweet smelling spiritual spices to flow. Yes, and now may God send forth his Word and may it make them flow in us."

Recluse or Reformer?

Born near Dijon in France's Burgundy region, Bernard (1090–1153) entered the new monastery of Citeaux in 1112, withdrawing from the world to devote himself to the worship of God and the practice of rigorous ascetical disciplines that left his body fragile and weak.

But he also felt called to play a role in matters outside the monastery walls. "From the moment he left the world, he tried to take the world with him into the monastery," wrote Adriaan H. Bredero. This integration of seclusion and engagement, devotion and action, would provide a model for many other monks and mystics of later centuries.

Monasteries underwent a series of reforms in the twelfth century (see sidebar), and Bernard was a reformer and loving critic of the Roman Catholic Church. Four centuries before a monk named Martin Luther broke with the church and led the Protestant Reformation, Bernard devoted much of his energy to reforming the monasteries and churches of his day. (Luther, Calvin, and other reformers later applauded his efforts. "I regard Bernard as the most pious of all the monks and prefer him to all the others," wrote Luther.)

By 1115, Bernard had demonstrated his abilities as a leader and preacher and was commissioned to found a new Cistercian monastery at Clairvaux. He served as the abbot there for the next thirty-eight years, and under his masterful guidance, Clairvaux itself helped found nearly seventy additional monasteries. Thanks to Bernard, the Cistercian movement rapidly spread throughout Europe. In Switzerland, a group of monks bred Saint Bernard dogs

Bernard and His Time

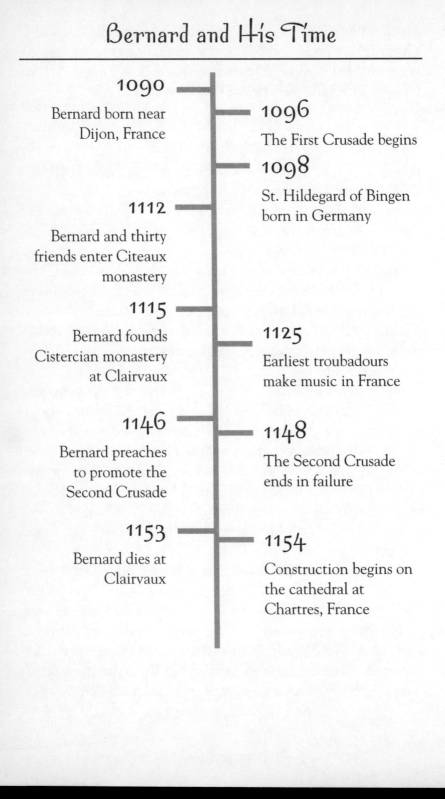

1090
Bernard born near
Dijon, France

1096
The First Crusade begins

1098
St. Hildegard of Bingen
born in Germany

1112
Bernard and thirty
friends enter Citeaux
monastery

1115
Bernard founds
Cistercian monastery
at Clairvaux

1125
Earliest troubadours
make music in France

1146
Bernard preaches
to promote the
Second Crusade

1148
The Second Crusade
ends in failure

1153
Bernard dies at
Clairvaux

1154
Construction begins on
the cathedral at
Chartres, France

that became famous for their ability to rescue travelers who became lost in the ferocious Alpine snowstorms.

Bernard's primary responsibility as an abbot was the spiritual care of his monks, and his daily lessons and sermons inspired many to put God first in their lives. As his life-long friend and biographer William of St. Thierry put it, "The first-fruits of his youth were dedicated to the work of restoring among his monks that fervor for the religious life which was found in the monks of Egypt long ago."

But there were times when this sweet-tongued preacher lashed out at the excesses he felt had corrupted spiritual practice in his day. In one case, he condemned churches that were too big, too wealthy, and decorated too elaborately.

> I will overlook the immense heights of the places of prayer, their immoderate lengths, their superfluous widths, the costly refinements, and the painstaking representations which deflect the attention . . . and thus hinder devotion. . . . I, however, say, "Tell me, poor man, if indeed you are poor men, what is gold doing in the holy place?"

As his reputation grew, his influence spread far beyond the walls of Clairvaux and the monasteries of the Cistercian order, drawing him into some of the larger issues of his day. He served as a peacemaker between warring political rulers. He helped heal the papal schism of the 1130s that saw two men duking it out for the right to be pope. And he publicly opposed a monk named Peter Abelard, a renowned scholar whose efforts to apply scientific thinking to the texts of the Bible troubled many church leaders.

In his most embarrassing public episode, Bernard helped rouse support for the Second Crusade—a horrible failure that resulted in the unnecessary loss of many lives. He also wrote the constitution for a new order—the Knights Templars—a band of Christian soldiers who both cared for the sick and gunned down infidels. Such saber rattling seems curious in a man like Bernard. But these were curious times, and only in later centuries would mystics like George Fox and Thomas Merton (see the later chapters on each of them) develop new ways of thinking about issues of war and peace.

A Lover Teaching the Way of Love

"You want me to tell you why God is to be loved and how much," wrote Bernard in his best-known work, *On Loving God.*

> I answer, the reason for loving God is God Himself; and the measure of love due to Him is immeasurable love. Is this plain?

> We are to love God for Himself, because of a twofold reason; nothing is more reasonable, nothing more profitable. When one asks, Why should I love God? he may mean, What is lovely in God? or What shall I gain by loving God? In either case, the same sufficient cause of love exists, namely, God Himself.

Love was such a central part of Bernard's life and thought that M. Basil Pennington, a modern-day Cistercian, called him "a lover teaching the way of love." In sermon after sermon, essay after essay, Bernard urged people to accept God's love and challenged them to give their own love back to God as best they could. He presents his case in *On Loving God:*

> Having written as best I can, though unworthily, of God's right to be loved, I have still to treat of the recompense which that love brings. For although God would be loved without respect of reward, yet He wills not to leave love unrewarded. True charity cannot be left destitute, even though she is unselfish and seeketh not her own [1 Corinthians 13:5].
>   Love is an affection of the soul, not a contract: it cannot rise from a mere agreement, nor is it so to be gained. It is spontaneous in its origin and impulse; and true love is its own satisfaction. It has its reward; but that reward is the object beloved. . . . True love does

not demand a reward, but it deserves one. Surely no one offers to pay for love; yet some recompense is due to one who loves, and if his love endures he will doubtless receive it.

Bernard's thoughts on love combined the esoteric otherworld-liness of supernatural compassion with the pragmatic this-worldli-ness of human nature. As he saw it, love was not only the key to understanding the Divine Creator but the only practical means of inspiring true change in human hearts.

> Neither fear nor self-interest can convert the soul. They may change the appearance, perhaps even the conduct, but never the object of supreme desire. . . . Fear is the motive which constrains the slave; greed binds the selfish man, by which he is tempted when he is drawn away by his own lust and enticed [James 1:14]. But neither fear nor self-interest is undefiled, nor can they convert the soul. Only charity can convert the soul freeing it from unwor-thy motives.

Loving God should come naturally, but it doesn't, so we need to learn how. Bernard taught that there are sequential steps in the growth of our love, beginning with our own selfish love of our-selves. Next comes a selfishly motivated love for God. Over time, this selfish love of God matures and we begin loving him for his own sake. "Our frequent needs oblige us to invoke God more often and approach him more frequently," writes Bernard. "This intimacy moves us to taste and discover how sweet the Lord is."

On Loving God may be Bernard's most popular work, but his *Sermons on the Song of Songs* is often praised as his mystical master-piece. At the time of his death, he was writing number 86 in this series of sermons for his monks that were based on King Solomon's passionate love poem. Bernard wasn't the first Christian writer to portray the exchanges between the poem's lovers as a metaphor for God's love for humanity, and he wouldn't be the last to do so. But his timeless and beautiful prose made him a favorite author for later mystics, many of whom employed breathless erotic language to describe their own transforming encounters with the Divine Lover.

In these sermons, Bernard describes stages by which our love for God can grow more intimate over time. Initially, many of us resemble the repentant sinner Mary Magdalene, who kissed the feet of Jesus and begged for mercy. Next, we kiss the hands of Jesus, inviting him to hold us and lift us up. Finally, we kiss the lips of Jesus. "For as you grow in grace and knock at the door with more assurance, you will seek for what is still lacking." Bernard says that when we kiss Jesus on the lips, we receive God's Spirit, which makes us one with our loving Creator. "The kiss of God is the gift of the Holy Spirit," he writes.

For Bernard, such spiritual communion is the true heart of the Christian life, and only in such communion can imperfect souls like ours find the true solace we desire. "God himself is love," he writes, "and nothing created can satisfy those who are made in the image of God except the God who is love."

But as long as we live in these earthly bodies, our communion with God will be only temporal and partial. Like a lover who misses an absent partner, we will long for more of God until our relationship with him can reach its ultimate consummation. "It is a happiness that is never complete, because the joy of his visit is followed by the pain of his departure," writes Bernard.

Expressing the Inexpressible

For nearly two thousand years, Christian mystics have struggled to describe their sublime supernatural experiences using humble human words that seem insufficient to the task. Thanks to his superior gifts with language, Bernard handled this challenge better than many. But even he struggled to express the inexpressible.

He often relied on biblical language like that found in the *Song of Songs*, in part because the Bible was an important part of his daily life. As a Cistercian monk, he spent more than half of each waking day reading, reciting, chanting, and meditating on biblical texts.

He also exhibited an innate ability to express complex mystical concepts through simple and concrete illustrations. Images of water appear frequently in his work, as they do in the work of later mystics. "As a drop of water seems to disappear completely in a big quantity of wine . . . so it is necessary for the saints that all human feelings melt in a mysterious way and flow into the will of God," he wrote.

On another occasion, he explained spiritual maturity by contrasting reservoirs with canals. It would be best, he said, if people resembled reservoirs, opening their souls to be filled with God's spirit and then allowing the overflow to empower their ministry to others. But instead, too many people resemble canals. The water of the Holy Spirit flows through their lives, but it disappears as soon as it arrives. "They want to pour it forth before they have been filled," he writes. "They are more ready to speak than to listen, impatient to teach what they have not grasped, and full of presumption to govern others while they know not how to govern themselves."

Bernard's own reservoir of spiritual experiences began filling up early. He was only a child when a Christmastime vision showing God becoming man and being born to the Virgin Mary gave him a lifelong fascination with the incarnation and a deep devotion to Mary.

Years later, another vision would confirm Bernard's calling as a preacher and abbot. The vision was described by friend and biographer, William of St. Thierry:

> As he stood still and closed his eyes for a moment in prayer, he saw coming down from the mountains round about him and down into the valley below such a great company of men of every type and standing that the valley could not hold them all.

Some mystics experience God through encounters that are disturbing or even violent, but Bernard's supernatural raptures were nearly always warm and affectionate, and he desired that others would come to know God as he had. "Learn, then, O Christian, from Christ the manner in which you ought to love Christ," he wrote. "Learn to love Him tenderly, to love Him wisely, to love Him with a mighty love."

And unlike vinegar-style preachers who try to keep people in line with threats of fire and brimstone, Bernard believed divine love could inspire ever-deeper devotion. "Nor do I think that when a soul has found Him will it cease from seeking," he wrote. "When a soul has been so blessed as to find Him, that secret desire is not extinguished, but on the contrary, it is increased."

Bernard's Twelve Steps to Spiritual Growth

Some of us think of mystics as people whose heads are in the clouds, and Bernard certainly had his moments of otherworldly rapture. But he was also an immensely practical man whose years as an abbot taught him much about how to counsel and guide the many monks who were under his care.

One of the illustrations he used in his teaching was the image of the ladder, which has been employed by mystics through the ages. But while mystics typically write about how to achieve spiritual maturity by ascending the ladder of growth, Bernard turned this simple illustration on its head in his insightful treatise, *The Steps of Humility and Pride*. "I could not very well describe the way up because I am more used to falling down than to climbing," he wrote. For those of us who want to grow closer to God but find many roadblocks and setbacks along the way, Bernard's advice on the steps *not* to take can help us avoid many of the spiritual life's most common snares and dead ends.

1. *Curiosity.* Bernard was a thoughtful, inquisitive person. So why did he call curiosity the first step on the ladder of pride? Because those who indulge in idle curiosity can become busybodies with short attention spans who spend more time condemning the faults of others than correcting our own recurring sins.

2. *Levity of mind.* Bernard didn't object to humor but had little patience with flighty, unstable people who were unable to make commitments and stick to them. "The eyes have wandered and the mind soon follows," he wrote, adding that spiritual growth comes more quickly to those who are calm and focused than to those who swing from "envious sadness" to "childish gladness."

3. *Giddiness.* Giddy souls have "retired into a happy cloudland," writes Bernard. "Vain thoughts and silly jokes gather pressure inside until they burst out in giggles."

4. *Boastfulness.* Some boasters like to teach others, but they're less interested in helping others than they are strutting their stuff before an appreciative audience. "Your hunger and thirst are for listeners."

5. *Singularity.* Image is everything for these deluded folks. "You do not so much want to be better as to be seen to be better," says Bernard.

6. *Self-conceit.* Those who lust after the praise of others often fail to examine their own motives or address their own faults.

7. *Presumption.* "When you think you are better than others will you not put yourself before others?" asks Bernard.

8. *Self-justification.* When caught in wrongdoing, self-justifiers engage in denial, claiming they were actually in the right or pleading that they meant well.

9. *Hypocritical confession.* Don't be fooled by downcast eyes full of tears. Proud people may look apologetic, but their penance is mainly for show and results in no long-term change.

10. *Revolt.* When things get so bad that spiritual companions or church leaders try to offer correction, the prideful resist any guidance but their own.

11. *Freedom to sin.* Following revolt becomes contempt for God. "They do not plunge headlong into the torrent of vice but feel their way step by step like one trying a ford."

12. *The habit of sinning.* First sins are indulged tentatively. But when lightning bolts fail to fall from the sky, temptations are embraced more heartily. "Sin is repeated and the pleasure grows," he writes. "Old desires revive, conscience is dulled, habit tightens its grip."

Bernard believed it was possible for people to experience a lifetime of humiliation without ever learning true humility, which he described as "a virtue by which one has a low opinion of one's self because one knows one's self well." But we can learn to grow in humility if we avoid falling down Bernard's steps to pride.

Cycles of Monastic Decline and Renewal

Things seemed so simple when Antony and the Desert Fathers founded their communities of prayer in the fourth century (see the second chapter). But as monasteries grew in number and size, many grew big and wealthy. Viking raiders who began rampaging through Europe in the ninth century targeted wealthy monasteries, which were easy targets laden with spoils.

By the time of Bernard, many Christian leaders felt that monasteries had gone off track and many monks had become fat and lazy. These reformers initiated a series of programs designed to return monasteries to a more pristine and rigorous lifestyle. Here's a brief survey of some of the key figures and movements.

Benedict. Benedict of Nursia was a hermit who founded the monastery of Monte Casino in Italy in 528. Before his death fifteen years later, he wrote a monastic Rule based on prayer, manual labor, and the vows of obedience, poverty, and chastity. Benedict's Rule is still followed in Benedictine monasteries and other communities around the world.

Cluny. The monastery of Cluny was founded in France in 910, and it gave birth to new monasteries and reformed older communities like Monte Casino. The Cluniac brothers were known as "Black Monks" because of their dark clothing.

A Soul Surrendered

Over the course of his life, Bernard created a wealth of insightful sermons, treatises, and books covering a wide range of subjects.

On one occasion, Bernard skillfully skewered human arrogance ("The man who is his own master is the disciple of a fool"). Elsewhere, he demonstrated a pastor's understanding of the wages of sin ("It is not as easy to climb out of a pit as to fall into one"). He also summarized centuries of theological debate on the conflict over grace and free will in six simple words ("To consent is to be saved"). And he gave us refreshingly commonsense advice for dealing with

---

Cistercians. After a while, even the Black Monks grew lax, and new reforms were proposed by "White Monks" known as Cistercians. Robert of Molesme, a Black Monk who became critical of Cluniac excesses, founded the monastery of Citeaux in 1098. Citeaux took the lead in the Cistercian reforms, and soon after Bernard joined this monastery in 1112, he became a leader in the movement.

Other reformers combined insights from the Desert Fathers and Benedict's Rule to create new movements such as the Camaldolese (founded by Romuald and Peter Damian, two monks from Ravenna) and the Carthusians (founded by the French monk Bruno). The Carmelites were founded in the thirteenth century.

Not all mystics were monks, but monasteries have continued to serve as havens for mystics through the ages. Teresa of Avila, John of the Cross, and Therese of Lisieux were Carmelites. Thomas Merton was a member of the Trappist order—a Cistercian reform movement. And Francis of Assisi and Ignatius of Loyola founded their own orders: the Franciscans and the Society of Jesus.

Today, the process of monastic reform continues in the many existing orders and through the creation of new movements like Teresa of Calcutta's Sisters of Charity.

life's trials and triumphs ("If things always went wrong, no one could endure it; if they always went well, one would become arrogant").

But Bernard's primary calling in life was to invite others to love God more fully, more deeply, and more selflessly. He was wise enough to know that many of us reach out to God only when our backs are against the wall and we need to be rescued. From the soldier in a foxhole praying that enemy bullets pass far over his head to the college student who probably should have spent more time studying for final exams, the heavens resound with prayers from people who want God to get them out of a jam, make them wealthy, or forgive them for sins they intend to commit again as soon as possible.

Bernard distinguished such self-centered prayers from the kind of prayers we pray when we really want to surrender ourselves to God's will, no matter what that might be. "God is not loved without our being rewarded for it," he wrote, "but He must be loved without concern for reward."

And since prayers of surrender don't come naturally to proud people like us, Bernard gave us a model to follow. We've shortened the prayer a bit (a lengthier version appears in James Houston's *The Love of God*), but if you want to begin moving beyond your own petty concerns to focus on a purer and deeper love for God, this brief prayer is an excellent place to start:

> Turn Yourself, O my God, toward me, so that You will enable me to be humble. Take wholly to Yourself the brief remainder of the years that belong to my poor life. My days have declined as a shadow, and they have perished without fruit. It is now impossible for me to recall them. But make me, in Your goodness, at least to meditate upon them before You in the bitterness of my soul. If there is anything in me that is not employed in Your service, remove it. O God, you know my simplicity. If it is the beginning of wisdom in recognizing my ignorance, then I realize that this is Your gift. Increase it in me I pray, so that I will not be ungrateful for the

least of Your benefits, but shall strive to supply that which is lacking in me. It is, then, for these Your benefits, that I love You with my feeble powers. Amen.

LEARNING MORE ABOUT
Bernard of Clairvaux

Bernard was a prolific writer, and the strong of heart can devour his collected *Works*, available from Cistercian Publications in Kalamazoo, Michigan. Those wanting less can find an excellent introduction to Bernard and selections from some of his key writings in *Bernard of Clairvaux: A Lover Teaching the Way of Love* (1997, New City Press), a compilation by M. Basil Pennington, who is a Cistercian monk at St. Joseph's Abbey in Spencer, Massachusetts.

Bernard's signature work is *The Love of God*, which is available in many translations and versions. Its popularity with evangelicals can be seen in James M. Houston's new translation, published as part of Multnomah's series, Classics of Faith & Devotion. Houston's version also features key writings by Bernard's lifelong friend, William of St. Thierry. *The Love of God* is also available in electronic versions, including *The Master Christian Library*, part of the AGES Digital Library (ageslibrary.com).

There are hundreds of Bernard biographies. An interesting addition to the literature is Adriaan H. Bredero's *Bernard of Clairvaux: Between Cult and History* (1996, Eerdmans), which seeks to separate hagiographic fantasy from historical fact.

Christian History magazine has also published a special issue devoted to Bernard (issue 24, christianhistory.net).

The Way of Visions
Hildegard of Bingen

The visions were intense and often overwhelming, and they began invading the soul of a young girl named Hildegard when she was only three years old. As the tenth child of well-to-do German parents, she was dedicated to God as a tithe, entering a Benedictine monastery at age eight. But she kept her visions to herself, as was appropriate for a woman growing up in the Middle Ages. After all, everyone knew women could be weak and easily confused. They shouldn't be trusted to convey divine truths. That was a man's job.

Everything changed when Hildegard was about forty-five years old. God spoke to her in a vision and commanded her to begin recording her visions and sharing the fruits of her experiences with the world. Hildegard always tried to obey God's promptings, no matter how crazy other people thought she was or how much trouble she caused, so she began writing down everything she saw in her private reveries.

She was still receiving visions as she entered her eighties, and throughout the second half of her life she kept a series of secretaries busy as she dictated accounts of her hundreds of excursions into the extraordinary. In some cases, she was transported to the future. At other times, she was given a front-row seat for witnessing events of the past. She was shown both the glories of heaven and the torments of hell. She was empowered to see deep into the souls of other people, including some of the less-than-saintly leaders of the Catholic Church—an institution she served as a loyal member all the days of her life. She was given insight into the cellular structure of plants, the anatomy of animals, and secret healing remedies.

And her spiritual journeys took her deep into the creative worlds of art, music, and language.

Some of her visions inspired her to write words and music she would sing with her fellow sisters. Other visions included divine instructions she was obligated to pass on to others, and she duly relayed these messages, regardless of whether they were full of cheer or condemnation and regardless of whether they were intended for wayward kings or sinful popes.

Some of the visions were beautiful and comforting; others were shocking and frightening. But after her otherworldly encounters, she usually felt strangely alive and deeply connected to God.

"I have never felt secure in my own abilities," she wrote in a letter to a monk named Guibert around the year 1175, four years before her death. "But I stretch out my hands to God, so that like a feather, which lacks all solidity of strength and flies on the wind, I may be sustained by him."

There are many ways to connect with God. Some people say they hear verbal messages. Others find comfort and guidance in sermons, books, intuitive impressions, or advice given by loving friends. But God apparently chose to communicate with Hildegard through visions, some of which came complete with blinding Technicolor™ images and thundering 1,000-watt sound.

"I see things," she told Guibert, a trusted friend and secretary during the later years of her life, "and I do not hear them with my bodily ears, nor with the thoughts of my heart, nor do I perceive them through a combination of my five senses, but ever in my soul, with my external eyes open, so that I never suffer debilitating ecstasy."

At times, the visions overpowered Hildegard's senses. "I see and hear and know at one and the same time," she wrote. "And the words which I see and hear in the vision are not like the words that sound from the mouth of man, but like a sparkling flame and a cloud moved by the pure air."

At other times, Hildegard caught a glimpse of something she called "the Living Light." She found it impossible to describe this image of the eternal God, but she sure knew how it made her feel. "While I behold it, all sadness and pain is lifted from my memory, so that I feel like a carefree young girl, and not the old woman that I am."

A Complex, Controversial Saint

Throughout her troubled and stormy life, Hildegard did her best to use her gifts for the glory of God and the service of the world. And even though she called herself a "poor little woman," she wasn't afraid to defy the sexual stereotypes of her age. She served as an abbess at her monastery and later founded two new monasteries of her own near Bingen. Her numerous preaching tours throughout her native German Rhineland area attracted large and passionate crowds, making her a kind of regional religious superstar.

Her growing fame and influence made Hildegard an easy target for her critics, most of them male leaders who didn't like her "haughty" manner or were jealous of her popularity and power. Some called her mad. Others said she was in league with the devil. But friends in high places, including the influential Bernard of Clairvaux, helped her out. Bernard, who exchanged letters with Hildegard after hearing about her visions, appealed to the Pope, who gave his seal of approval to her writings.

At the time of her death, Hildegard was a celebrated seer. But after her death, she seemed to fade from people's memory and the historical record of her time. Perhaps it was because Germany was experiencing a mini-renaissance that witnessed an explosion of bold new thinkers and daring new ideas. Perhaps it was because her writings were so dense and inscrutable that few could figure out what she was saying. Perhaps it was because a charismatic young Italian mystic named Francis of Assisi, who was born two years after Hildegard died, would quickly turn Europe's religious scene on its head.

It would be centuries before Hildegard became famous once again. Interest began picking up again around 1979—the year

Hildegard and Her Time

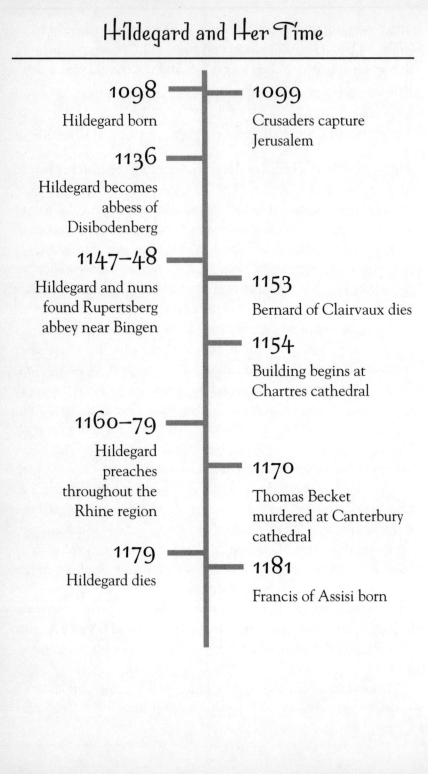

1098
Hildegard born

1099
Crusaders capture
Jerusalem

1136
Hildegard becomes
abbess of
Disibodenberg

1147–48
Hildegard and nuns
found Rupertsberg
abbey near Bingen

1153
Bernard of Clairvaux dies

1154
Building begins at
Chartres cathedral

1160–79
Hildegard
preaches
throughout the
Rhine region

1170
Thomas Becket
murdered at Canterbury
cathedral

1179
Hildegard dies

1181
Francis of Assisi born

many small but devoted groups of scholars and nuns around the world celebrated the eight hundredth anniversary of her death. Soon a growing number of people were rediscovering the Rhineland mystic and embracing different portions of her complex legacy.

In the 1980s, a defrocked Dominican priest and apostle of "Creation Spirituality" named Matthew Fox wrote books about Hildegard. Meanwhile, other spiritual seekers and disciples of alternative spirituality applauded Hildegard as a potent seer who transcended the narrow doctrinal confines of the Christian creeds. Feminists embraced her as a pioneer of women's equality. Natural health aficionados pored over her fascinating works on medicinal plants and healing techniques. And musicians dusted off her old musical compositions, combining her ethereal words with world beat rhythms and electronic musical accompaniments.

By the time English author Fiona Maddocks finished her biography of Hildegard in 2001, the Rhineland saint was awash in "a flood of misappropriation and fabulous invention." Maddocks complained about those who transformed Hildegard into the patron saint of their pet causes. "As a quick look at the Internet shows, she has become the darling of crankish cults and New Age zealots, Creationists and Greens, women's movements and alternative doctors."

Always complex and often confusing, Hildegard is as little understood in our day as she was in her own. And I must confess that I find much of the recent Hildegard hoopla a bit off-putting. As a result, I had never read much about her until my coauthor encouraged me to do so. Since learning more about her, I have been inspired by her life and hope you will find her encouraging as well.

Sights and Sounds from Out of This World

"I was only in my third year when I saw a heavenly light which made my soul tremble," says Hildegard in her *Vita* (or official biography), "but because I was a child I could not speak out."

Visions were such a normal part of her life that it took her a while to realize that others didn't experience the same things she did. "I tried to find out from my nurse if she saw anything at all other than the usual external objects." But when the nurse reported she hadn't seen anything out of the ordinary, Hildegard became even more committed to secrecy. "Then I was seized with a great fear and did not dare to reveal this to anyone."

Some parents pressure their children to be normal, but Hildegard's mother and father saw the big soul in the small child; they placed her in the Disibodenberg monastery where Hildegard would later experience one of the most profound visions of her life.

"I saw an extremely strong, sparkling, fiery light coming from the open heavens," she recalled later. "It pierced my brain, my heart and my breast through and through like a flame which did not burn. . . . And suddenly I had an insight into the meaning and interpretation of the Psalter, the Gospel and the other catholic writings of the Old and New Testaments."

Hildegard was later named the abbess of Disibodenberg, but physical ailments often left her weak and frail. She was nearly forty-five when a voice from heaven commanded her to go public with her private inner life:

> O frail mortal, ashes of ashes and dust of dust, say and write what you see and hear. But since you are fearful of speaking, artless at explaining and untaught in writing, speak and write not according to human words nor following the understanding of human intelligence, nor according to the rules of human composition, but according to what you see and hear in the heavens above and in God's wondrous works.

For the remaining four decades of her life, Hildegard and her loyal secretaries, including Volmar—a devout and devoted monk—wrote down everything she could recall of her life story and her many visions. Making her once-private inner life public was a major transition for Hildegard. And even though she could never figure out whether to call her experiences perceptions, illumina-tions, or visionary insights, she shared them with the world.

> And I heard and wrote them not according to the invention of my
> own or anyone else's heart, but as I saw, heard and understood them
> in heavens, through the secret mysteries of God. And again I heard
> the voice from Heaven saying to me: "Proclaim and write thus."

Illuminating Manuscripts

Relieved of the obligation to remain silent, Hildegard started speaking about her visions. Her words would soon fill the pages of numerous theological and biographical books.

One of Hildegard's most popular works was *Scivias*, which means "know the ways" or "know God's ways." The book contains more than two dozen visions, including scenes of Satan being booted out of heaven, images of the three persons of the Holy Trin-ity sharing "the most sweet liquor of holiness," visions of the holy church bathing in the blood of its Redeemer, and premonitions of the Last Days, which Hildegard believed were right around the cor-ner. As she saw it, earthly history was divided into seven distinct periods. "But now," she says, "the world is in the seventh age, approaching its end, just as it were the seventh day."

Another work, *The Book of Life's Merits*, records strange and fascinating visions that describe dozens of human vices with the help of images that blend features from the natural world with oth-erworldly scenes. *The Book of Divine Works* is even more complex and dazzling. It takes a cosmic view of the work of the Creator, who "established the pillars that uphold the entire globe." In one color-ful vision, Hildegard sees a volcano. Her description is typical of those found in some of her more colorful works:

> And again I saw, as it were, a four-square apparition like a great city,
> walled alternately with brightness and darkness and furnished with
> certain mountains and figures. And I saw in the middle of its eastern

region something like a great broad mountain of hard white stone, like a volcano in form, at whose summit a mirror of such bright purity shone forth that it seemed to outshine the sun. In it the image of a dove appeared with wings outspread ready to fly. And the same mirror held within many hidden mysteries and gave out a brightness of great breadth and height, in which many mysteries and many forms of diverse figures appeared.

Hildegard also saw visions of a Cosmic Man, a Cosmic Egg, and many other puzzling entities. Some of the nuns who lived in her monastery and worked in its scriptorium attempted to translate some of her fantastic visions into paintings that were published along with Hildegard's texts. A surprising number of these psychedelic illustrations have survived, and they offer deeper insights into the saint's often perplexing visions, even if they fail to answer all the questions we might have about their meaning.

Australian scholar Sabina Flanagan has spent much of her adult life studying Hildegard's amazing and often baffling works. She even translated some of the saint's writings from Latin into English. But she still isn't sure she always grasped what Hildegard was trying to say. "I am not sure that I have always managed to capture her exact meaning," confesses Flanagan in her introduction to her 1996 collection, *Secrets of God: Writings of Hildegard of Bingen.*

Earthly Advice

Not all of Hildegard's visions were so otherworldly or so difficult to interpret. One vision that came to her often featured a group of virgins dancing together as they worshipped God. *Scivias* includes a description of one of these virginal visions:

> Among them I saw, as in a mirror, some who were all dressed in whitest garments; some of them had a circlet shining like the dawn on their heads, and their shoes were whiter than snow.

Hildegard's interpretation of this vision was straightforward. She believed God had given her specific guidelines about how she and her nuns should dress and worship. After she turned fifty and founded the first of two monasteries near the town of Rupertsberg near Bingen on the Rhine River, Hildegard and her eighteen sisters sewed clothing that resembled the garments she had seen in her vision and enacted some of the dances she had witnessed the heavenly virgins enjoying.

Her visions were not always so comforting. Hildegard spent much of her life in a state of perpetual anxiety and agitation. This, along with her strict ascetic practices of fasting and self-punishment, resulted in a lifetime of health problems and migraine headaches. It's not surprising, then, that some of the visions she received dealt with healing remedies that could benefit her and others who, when sick, faced two equally unattractive options: suffering in silence or going to a medieval "doctor" whose treatment might cause more harm than good. As God told her in *Scivias:* "I am the great Physician of all diseases and act like a doctor who sees a sick man who longs to be cured."

Undergirding Hildegard's health-related visions was the deep belief that there was a God-ordained harmony existing throughout all of creation. "God fashioned the human form according to the constitution of the firmament and of all other creatures," she said.

Many of Hildegard's healing visions were collected in two books that are avidly read today by all manner of spiritual healers and are readily available under a number of creative titles that reveal at least some of their contents: *Causes and Cures, Book of Simple Medicine*, or even *Hildegard's Apothecary*.

There's scant scientific verification of Hildegard's prescriptions, and many Western doctors dismiss her many potions and cures as the misinformed imaginings of a well-meaning but overly excited Dark Ages nun. But that hasn't stopped many from following her suggestions for using herbs like lavender ("it will soften the pain in the liver") or minerals like sapphire ("the stone of wisdom and intelligence that gives a clear mind by its power"). Today, many alternative healers agree with Hildegard's claim: "These remedies come from God."

Even more controversial was Hildegard's dispensation of detailed advice on sex. Some of her male critics charged that she possessed more knowledge about the subject than was appropriate for a nun sworn to lifelong virginity.

But whenever she was under the gun, she deflected her critics' complaints, claiming she was not the source of her teachings but merely a messenger. "I am a poor earthen vessel," she said, "and say these things not of myself but from the serene Light."

Music of the Spheres

Hildegard's work as an abbess, an author, an adviser, a healer, a preacher, and a seer would be enough to guarantee her a place in the mystics' hall of fame. But one other fascinating aspect of this complex woman inspires curiosity and awe: Hildegard was a musical composer, which because of my interest in music intrigues me even more. Soon after she was elected abbess of Disibodenberg, she began writing songs for her nuns to sing. Nearly eighty of her compositions have survived the centuries intact, and now vocal ensembles around the world are performing her music once again, making Hildegard one of the most popular medieval musicians.

Just as Hildegard's healing visions illustrated her view that God was the Divine Creator who reigned supreme over the natural and supernatural worlds, her mystical music reflected her belief that God was the Divine Artist who first spoke the cosmos into existence and now sustains it with the sound of his voice.

Barbara Thornton is the director of Sequentia—an ensemble that performs and records medieval music. *Canticles of Ecstasy*—Sequentia's 1994 recording of some of Hildegard's music—includes an essay by Thornton on the theology reflected in the saint's compositions. "She called them *symphoniae harmoniae celestium revelationum*," wrote Thornton—"a title meant to indicate their divine inspiration as well as the idea that music is the highest form of human activity, mirroring as it does the ineffable sounds of heavenly spheres and angel choirs."

Or as Hildegard herself put it:

> Every element has a sound, an original sound from the order of God; all those sounds unite like the harmony from harps and zithers. Those voices you hear are like the voice of a multitude, which lifts its sound on high; for jubilant praises, offered in simple harmony and charity, lead the faithful to that consonance in which is no discord, and make those who still live in earth sigh with heart and voice for the heavenly reward.

There's even a legend that papal investigators researching whether or not Hildegard should be canonized interviewed three of the nuns in her community after her death. The nuns reported seeing their abbess after she died. She was moving through the cloister late at night chanting "O Virga Ac Diadema" (Praise for the Mother), one of the songs she had written. The sisters said that as she chanted, she gave off a heavenly glow.

Hildegard's songs, which were inspired by her visions and composed for the sisters' corporate worship, cover many of the key themes found in other liturgical music. In addition to numerous songs dedicated to the Virgin Mary, there were compositions celebrating the incarnation of Christ ("O vis aeternitatis"), the ministry of the Holy Spirit ("Spiritus Sanctus vivificans vita"), and numerous songs about her blessed virgins. One song about the virgins ("O noblissima viriditas") includes concise references to some of the visual elements of her visions:

> *You glow red like the dawn,*
> *and you burn like the sun's fire.*

Though the lyrics often came first, Hildegard said the compositions weren't complete until this basic structure was clothed with celestial music. "When the words come, they are merely empty shells without the music," she says. "They live as they are sung, for the words are the body and the music the spirit."

Throughout much of Hildegard's music, certain musical themes appear time and time again. In some of her improvisations, these

---

Loves Human and Divine

Rules governing monastic communities have long warned against developing "particular friendships" that lead members to favor some people over others. Benedict's Rule addresses this matter in simple but direct language: "Let him not love one more than another."

Although some people might find such warnings archaic or puritanical, they illustrate a deeper truth I have observed in our own community—The Brothers and Sisters of Charity. To enter fully into communal life requires that we must make a clean break from flawed patterns of past relationships. And commands about "particular friendships" are designed to inspire authentic community relationships and true spiritual friendships by removing the obstacles that result from "exclusive" approaches toward relationships.

Hildegard followed these simple commands for most of the seven decades she lived the religious life, but her deep affection for a daughter of nobility named Richardis von Stade violated this principle and at least temporarily threw Hildegard's life into confusion.

After being a member of Hildegard's monastery and working with Volmar as a secretary, Richardis decided to leave and serve as the abbess of another monastery. The decision shocked Hildegard, who had grown closer to Richardis than perhaps she had realized.

Hildegard responded by condemning the younger nun's decision, telling others that it was the result of devilish pride, not godly central musical motifs can be demanding for contemporary singers. For example, one piece featured an elaborate melisma extending over seventy-five notes. Such cases show why these compositions often sound like an ethereal hybrid of Gregorian chant and Joni Mitchell.

submission. "She did not seek this however, according to God, but according to this world's honor," she wrote.

When Hildegard's archbishop wrote and instructed her to let the girl go, the saint responded in the most unsaintly manner. "Your malicious curses and threatening words are not to be obeyed," she wrote to the archbishop. "These legal pretexts brought forward to establish authority over this girl have no weight in God's eyes."

Ultimately, Richardis left, with Hildegard predicting her imminent doom for doing so. About two years after her departure, the younger nun died very suddenly. Scholars have had a field day with the whole episode. Some have even declared that the two women were involved in a homosexual relationship—a conclusion that is dismissed by most researchers.

Still, there may be valuable lessons to be learned from this friendship gone sour. One lesson is that St. Benedict's admonition against favoritism in faith communities may be a wiser piece of advice than many of us realize. Christian communities can be tested or weakened by inappropriate relationships and dependencies.

The Richardis episode also conveys a second valuable lesson about the pervasiveness of human fallibility, even among the faith's recognized saints and mystics. Hildegard's willingness to wrap herself in the mantle of the godly mystic and do battle with anyone who disagreed with her shows that no matter how many heavenly experiences we have, we still remain people with clay feet planted firmly in this world of imperfection and half-truth.

Hildegard's complex and varied work illustrates what might be called a metaphysical understanding of the close interdependence of color, sound, rhythms, harmonies, and other elements that make up God's divine music and art. Each one of these elements has a unique impact on our emotions, even the various organs of our body. That's why some music assists in the process of healing.

And according to the *Grove Dictionary of Music and Musicians*, Hildegard created "the earliest morality play by more than a century." Morality plays, which became increasingly popular during later centuries, were dramatic presentations featuring actors personifying Christian virtues like humility or purity. Though tempted by the devil, the godly characters in Hildegard's dramas ultimately remained faithful to God.

Under Divine Control

Visions have played a powerful role in my own life. Both my work as a community founder and as a musician and composer of contemporary sacred music were based on a vision I received in 1971. I also experienced other visions of a more personal nature that inspired my conversion and subsequent vocational journey. Perhaps it is because of these experiences and my love of sacred music that I find Hildegard so interesting.

Some call Hildegard a genius. Others say she was a pre-Renaissance renaissance woman or creative polymath. But as she saw it, she was merely a simple woman in thrall to a much higher power. A feather on the breath of God, she went first this way and then that way, following the promptings of her Heavenly Father and going wherever he guided her.

When you think about it, that's not a bad goal for any of us who desire to experience a powerful connection with God in our own lives. But how do we do that? How do we order our lives in such a way that God can prompt and guide us?

We can't pretend to be Hildegard, and we shouldn't waste time trying to imagine that our twenty-first century is like her twelfth century. But in our own lives and our own time, we can seek to cultivate the wholehearted love and single-minded focus she had for God. It might also help if we could turn down the chaotic noise of our lives so that we might be able to hear when God's still, small voice speaks to our soul.

Perhaps if we maintain an attitude of hopeful silence and keep our heart open to the breath of God, we too can see some of the things Hildegard saw, hear some of the words she heard, and experience just a small portion of the heavenly love that she knew so well for so long.

LEARNING MORE ABOUT
Hildegard of Bingen

There has been a revival of interest in Hildegard of late, resulting in a bumper crop of books by and about this unique saint. As with the work of many other mystics, her best-known work *(Scivias)* is available in Paulist Press's Classics of Western Spirituality series. And lesser-known works are available in English today that were impossible to find a quarter century ago.

But if you're just beginning to explore Hildegard, the best place to begin is Sabina Flanagan's *Secrets of God: Writings of Hildegard of Bingen*, which was published in the United States in 1996 by Shambhala Publications, which is best known for its works on Buddhism. The collection includes portions of most of her major works and includes four-color reproductions of some of the illustrations created by artists during the saint's lifetime. Flanagan also wrote the biography, *Hildegard of Bingen: A Visionary Life* (Routledge, 1989).

A more recent biography is Fiona Maddocks's *Hildegard of Bingen: The Woman of Her Age* (Doubleday, 2001)—a well-written study that incorporates some of the latest research.

Barbara Newman, another of the better-known scholars, has written numerous books about Hildegard, including *Sister of Wisdom: St. Hildegard's Theology of the Feminine* (University of California Press, 1997).

If you want to listen to some of Hildegard's music while you're reading, you have your choice from more than a half-dozen CDs, including Sequentia's *Canticles of Ecstasy* (which seeks to recreate the compositions in their original style) and Richard Souther's *Vision: The Music of Hildegard of Bingen*. The popular 1994 album, which attempts to update these medieval compositions by giving them a contemporary-music sheen, was released by Angel, the same label that had an earlier surprise multiplatinum success with *Chant*, an album of Gregorian hymns.

I address topics related to mysticism and music more fully in my books, *Music of Creation, Come to the Quiet*, and *The Joy of Music Ministry*.

The Way of Joy
Francis of Assisi

Late one moonlit night, the citizens of Assisi, Italy, were awakened from their slumber by a frightful commotion. The cause of the disturbance was a local youth named Francis, but none of the townspeople realized that yet. All they knew was that the bells of their town church were clanging chaotically in the middle of the night.

These were the same bells that sounded throughout the daylight hours, chiming out familiar tones at morning, noon, and dusk. But this wasn't daylight, and this noise was no pretty melody. It sounded like a pack of hyenas had been let loose in the bell tower.

When a few droopy-eyed town fathers made their way to the central square in their nightshirts and slippers, they were greeted with a surreal sight. Francis was yanking on the bells' thick ropes with all his might and shouting out through the tower's windows: "Lift up your eyes, my friends! Lift up your eyes! Look at the moon!"

This wasn't the first time Francis had disturbed the sleep of his fellow townspeople. He had been a medieval party animal whose carousing, drinking, and loud singing were regular features of Assisi nightlife. But it wasn't drunken debauchery that inspired this outburst. On this moonlit night, Francis was fueled by a passionate love for God—a love so surpassing, so consuming, so glorious, and so transforming that he felt it was his duty to share it with his entire town.

A Joyful Saint

Some of the saints and mystics we see pictured in stained-glass windows or described in devotional books appear somber and lifeless. Such otherworldly portrayals can make holy men and women look more like angels than full-blooded figures who laughed, cried, had bad breath, or experienced mood swings. These two-dimensional holy men and women seem so completely absorbed in heavenly bliss that their feet barely touch the earth.

Not so with St. Francis of Assisi (who was born in either 1181 or 1182 and died in 1226), whose infectious, passionate, no-holds-barred love for God ignited a small band of followers that grew into a fellowship of thousands by the time of his death. Today, more than a million people around the globe follow Francis, the world's most beloved saint.

Although some saints are enshrined in stained glass and others look down at us from imposing statues or paintings, Francis is most frequently memorialized in bird feeders that show him caring for God's feathered creatures.

Francis is also remembered for a brief sermon he gave, but unlike some of history's most renowned speeches, Francis's sermon wasn't even intended for a human audience, the way, for example, Winston Churchill's rousing World War II speeches, John F. Kennedy's 1961 inaugural address, or the famous "I have a dream" speech by Martin Luther King Jr. were. Francis had other listeners in mind.

He delivered his most famous sermon on a crisp spring day when he and a few of his brothers were traveling through the beautiful Spoleto valley near the town of Bevagna. According to a brother who recorded what happened, Francis looked up and saw the trees full of doves, crows, and daws. Francis "left his companions in the road and ran eagerly toward the birds" and "humbly begged them to listen to the word of God." His sermon petitions his winged friends to acknowledge their Maker:

My brothers, birds, you should praise your Creator very much and always love him; he gave you feathers to clothe you, wings so that you can fly, and whatever else was necessary for you. God made you noble among his creatures, and he gave you a home in the purity of the air; though you neither sow nor reap, he nevertheless protects and governs you without any solicitude on your part.

Later, Thomas of Celano would write that the birds stretched their necks and extended their wings as Francis walked among them, touching and blessing them. Francis was so pleased with the birds' response that he resolved to preach more sermons of this type. "He began to blame himself for negligence in not having preached to the birds before," writes Thomas, and "from that day on, he solicitously admonished all birds, all animals and reptiles, and even creatures that have no feeling, to praise and love their Creator."

Francis loved God so completely that he wanted all of creation to join him in his celebration. That's why he once spoke to a brightly colored field of flowers: "He preached to them and invited them to praise the Lord as if they were endowed with reason," wrote a biographer.

Francis wasn't indulging in some kind of quaint, primitive anthropomorphism. Rather, this simple man who would later be named the patron saint of the environmental movement was merely urging each and every created thing to experience the joy of its Creator and express this joy in its own unique way:

In the same way he exhorted with the sincerest purity cornfields and vineyards, stones and forests and all the beautiful things of the fields, fountains of water and the green things of the gardens, earth and fire, air and wind, to love God and serve him willingly.

A Life Lived for God

Like many of the most celebrated mystics, Francis lived at a time when great social and spiritual upheaval forced people to cast themselves on the mercies of God. In Italian towns like Assisi,

Francis and His Time

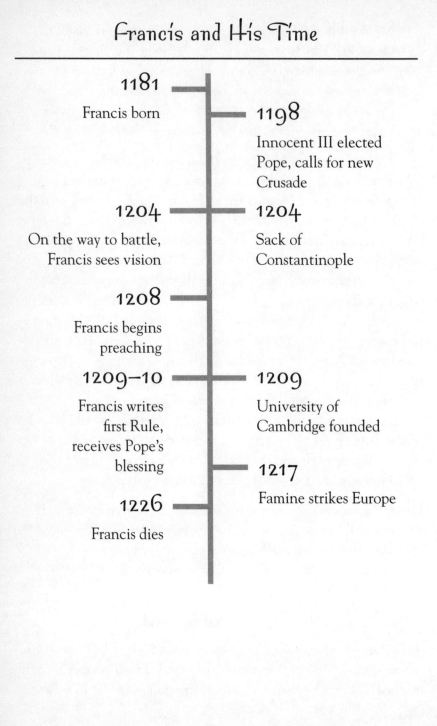

1181

Francis born

1198

Innocent III elected Pope, calls for new Crusade

1204

On the way to battle, Francis sees vision

1204

Sack of Constantinople

1208

Francis begins preaching

1209–10

Francis writes first Rule, receives Pope's blessing

1209

University of Cambridge founded

1217

Famine strikes Europe

1226

Francis dies

merchants like Francis's father were being linked to other businesses around the world in a network of trade and commerce that created unimagined wealth and unprecedented disparities between rich and poor.

At the same time, the church of Francis's day was a big, wealthy, bureaucratically entrenched and politically powerful institution whose leaders often seemed more like grasping, self-centered potentates than selfless servants of God and humanity.

Before his dramatic change of life, Francis had enjoyed a life of ease and luxury. One biographer described him as "vain and proud" and a "master of revels" who "squandered and wasted his time miserably." When he volunteered to fight in one of the frequent wars between Italian towns, he was captured before he fired his first shot and was put in prison, where he was held for a year until his father paid a hefty ransom. After his release, Francis made one more effort to fight in battle, but his plans were interrupted by the first in a series of supernatural visions. He returned home confused and disoriented. He thought God might be trying to tell him something, and he visited a small, run-down chapel located outside Assisi. While praying there, Francis heard the voice of Jesus speaking to him from a crucifix: "Francis, go, repair my house, which, as you see, is falling completely into ruin."

He didn't stop to question the words, and he didn't calculate what it might cost him to obey them. Instead he turned away from his comfortable life and threw himself into renovating the chapel. When conflicts with his father escalated, the man disowned Francis. "Until now I called you my father," said Francis. "But from now on I can say without reserve, 'Our Father Who art in heaven.' "

Francis was particularly sensitive to Jesus' words about the temptations of wealth and the need for compassionate service to the weak and the needy. He gave away everything he owned and adopted a lifestyle of poverty, simplicity, and service.

His parents and the other residents of Assisi were aghast at his radical faith. Why had this merchant's son traded his fashionable clothes for the rags of a beggar man? What was this former playboy doing hanging out with those lepers? Had he lost his mind? Had he suffered brain damage in the war?

Perhaps we would have thought Francis mad, too, but looking back on it all now, it seems God may have reached out to Francis at a time when the church was becoming cold and dead. Francis embraced the divine summons, and he responded by lighting a bonfire of burning love for God that still warms us today across these many centuries.

Seeing the Creator in All Creation

God is the biggest mystery in this whole perplexing world of ours. As a result, some people only grasp bits and pieces of God's character, while others misunderstand him altogether.

In the 1950s, Anglican writer J. B. Phillips wrote a book called *Your God Is Too Small* that described some of the most common false impressions. Phillips said many adults cling to "the conception of God that exists in the mind of a child of Sunday-school age." Some picture a "resident policeman" who punishes them with guilt and unhappiness. Others imagine a "parental hangover" who is little more than a warmed-over image of their mothers or fathers. Still others see God as a Grand Old Man in the sky who feels much more comfortable with chariots and togas than he does automobiles and slacks.

Phillips was right. Our image of God plays a powerful role in our relationship with God. And if there's one thing that's clear about Francis's theology, it's that he had a very big view of a very big God. Francis's theology shaped the way he saw the world, and the way he saw the world shaped his concept of the Creator.

It was St. Bonaventure—one of the most important early Franciscan leaders—who best described this important aspect of Francis's faith:

> In beautiful things St. Francis saw Beauty itself, and through His vestiges imprinted on creation he followed his Beloved everywhere,

making from all things a ladder by which he could climb up and embrace Him who is utterly desirable.

Bonaventure explored the key concepts of Franciscan spirituality in his classic book, *The Journey of the Mind to God.* "The created world is itself a ladder leading us to God," he wrote. Bonaventure said people could find traces of God by looking "outside" to creation and "inside" our own souls. This leads us to look "up" to find God in himself.

As Bonaventure saw it, creation was the bottom rung of a ladder that can lead us to God. "Whoever is not enlightened by such brilliance of things created must be blind," he wrote. "Whoever is not awakened by their mighty voice must be deaf. Whoever fails to praise God for all his works must be dumb. Whoever fails to discover the First Principle through all these signs must be a fool."

So we can see that Francis was more than a simple nature lover or a tree-hugger. He was a man who allowed God to touch his heart through the beauty of the created world.

Centuries after the saint's death, his hometown of Assisi still honors his affection for winged creatures. There, as in other towns, church bells ring three times a day to announce the Angelus—an ancient Christian prayer that honors the incarnation of Jesus. In Assisi, the reciting of this prayer is accompanied by the feeding of Francis's beloved birds.

And it's not just Assisi that honors Francis's deep love for creation. Every year on the Sunday nearest his October 4th feast day, thousands of Catholic, Episcopalian, and Protestant churches around the world host services in which animals are blessed. Some believers within those traditions still can't get over the sight of people bringing their dogs, cats, and parrots to church, but these services are a wonderful way to celebrate both Francis's and God's compassionate concern for all creatures.

Different people have different means they use to bring God to mind so they can focus on him as they pray and meditate. For example, Eastern Orthodox churches are adorned with icons of saints that serve as windows to God for worshippers. For Francis, all of creation was one gigantic icon that revealed the love, mercy, power, and majesty of his Heavenly Father. Through these works of the Creator, Francis's love for God grew deeper.

The Franciscan Way of Prayer

It's not surprising that when Brother Boniface Maes wrote his book *Franciscan Mysticism*, he often resorted to images of nature to describe God's grace. In one passage, Maes used the metaphor of the river:

> The grace of God sometimes overflows like a river and invades the emotional powers of the soul . . . there follows spiritual intoxication, which is a breaking out of overwhelming tenderness and delicious intimacies greater than the heart can desire or contain.

It's not surprising to see Maes talk about the river of God's grace, but some readers may be surprised to hear a Franciscan author using terms like *intoxication* and *intimacies* to describe the relationship between human and God. But such passionate language is a hallmark of Franciscan spirituality. Franciscan friar Raymond Lull titled his manual on prayer *The Book of the Lover and the Beloved*—a title that I borrowed for my own book on Franciscan prayer, *The Lover and the Beloved*.

Francis never wrote much, but accounts of his life make it clear that he embraced a bride-bridegroom approach to mysticism that his followers later developed more fully. He often spoke of his relationship with God as wedded bliss, and his radically simple lifestyle sprang from his love for something he called Lady Poverty.

People who think mysticism is complex and confusing may gain refreshingly simple insight from the Franciscans, who for centuries have taught that the mystical love union that grows between God and his people happens in much the same way that a human love relationship grows over time. And as any couple knows, time spent alone together helps intimacies deepen and mature.

Francis was active with his brothers and in various forms of public ministry, but he jealously guarded his time alone with God, much the way a lover protects her intimate moments with her partner. Biographies of the saint are brimming over with colorful descriptions of the lengths to which Francis would go to be alone in God's presence, as well as pictures of the way this deep spiritual intimacy affected his entire life.

One time when Francis was visiting a friend near the Lake of Perugia, he felt an inner nudging to go away and be alone with God. He asked his friend to take him to a solitary island in the lake and asked that the friend return to pick him up after forty days. Once on the island, which had no buildings, Francis found a dense thicket of thorn bushes and small trees where he made a simple shelter. As a biographer tells us: "He began to pray and contemplate heavenly things in that place."

But Francis realized that his calling to minister to others made it impractical for him and his followers to disappear into the wilderness for weeks at a time. That's why he founded two dozen hermitages during his life, creating havens for intense spiritual intimacy in the Italian countryside.

Throughout Christian history, people have gone to great lengths to create monasteries and hermitages in out-of-the-way places. For example, the islands off the coasts of Greece and Ireland are home to extremely isolated sites of prayer and meditation. But Franciscan hermitages were different. They were distant enough from population centers so the brothers could enjoy silence and solitude with God, but they were close enough to towns that the brothers were not so isolated that they were unable to serve others.

The brothers in Francis's new movement lived in an ongoing tension between their desire to be alone with God and their desire to serve their neighbors. But there were times when Francis preferred to be with his God. One biographer described the saint's attitude toward these intense times of prayer: "Francis was often suspended in such sweetness of contemplation that, caught up out of himself, he could not reveal what he had experienced because it went beyond all human comprehension."

Joy in the Face of Sorrow

Francis was a joyful saint, but that doesn't mean he was always happy or that his love for God depended on rosy circumstances. One bitterly cold winter day, Francis and a friar, Brother Leo, were returning to a monastery named St. Mary of the Angels after visiting a nearby town. Francis used the lengthy walk as an opportunity to teach Brother Leo that perfect joy wasn't to be found in positive outcomes like the success of the Franciscan movement, or the ability to perform amazing miracles, or the possession of vast knowledge, or the ability to preach with such beauty and effectiveness that all who heard would be converted.

After a few more miles of such lectures, Brother Leo became curious and asked, "Father, I beg you in God's name to tell me what perfect joy is." St. Francis replied:

> When we come to St. Mary of the Angels, soaked by the rain and frozen by the cold, all soiled with mud and suffering from hunger, and we ring at the gate of the place and the brother porter comes and says angrily: "Who are you?" And we say: "We are two of your brothers." And he contradicts us, saying, "You are not telling the truth. Rather you are two rascals who go around deceiving people and stealing what they give to the poor. Go away!" And he does not open for us, but makes us stand outside in the snow and rain, cold and hungry, until night falls—then if we endure all those insults and cruel rebuffs patiently, without being troubled and without complaining, and if we reflect humbly and charitably that the porter really knows us and that God makes him speak against us, oh, Brother Leo, write that perfect joy is there!

Francis wasn't a masochist, but he understood that affliction could teach us much about love, patience, humility, and service to others. "Above all the graces and gifts of the Holy Spirit which Christ gives to his friends is that of conquering oneself and willingly enduring suffering, insults, humiliations, and hardships for the love of Christ," he said.

Francis would have understood what twentieth-century thinker Eric Hoffer meant when he said, "The search for happiness is one of the chief sources of unhappiness." Francis didn't search for happiness, and, as a result, happiness seemed to come his way. Or, as St. Bonaventure put it, "Francis was at peace in his utter loyalty to God and he felt a heavenly joy in his heart which showed in his face, even in the midst of his tears."

Francis's Canticle of Love

Earlier in this chapter, I mentioned that many churches host services commemorating Francis that feature the blessing of animals. Many of these services use Francis's famous "Canticle of Brother Sun."

The canticle is a beautiful piece of poetry that describes many of the glories of the natural world. We might imagine that Francis wrote it while sitting on a rocky Italian hilltop on a warm, sunny day. Perhaps he was even enjoying a picnic and munching on grapes as he composed the poem's verses.

But such a fantasy doesn't reflect the reality of the canticle's composition. Francis wrote the poem late in his life. Blindness had cut him off from the outside world, so the descriptions of nature in the poem come from his memory. Francis's harsh regime of penitence and fasting had left his body weak and worn. In addition, by this time in his life Francis had received the stigmata.

The stigmata were physical wounds on Francis's hands, feet, and abdomen that mirrored the wounds Christ suffered during his crucifixion. There is much debate about the stigmata, which Francis tried to conceal from his brothers. But I believe they reflect the fact that his mystical union with Christ included a spiritual union with the crucified Christ, which resulted in these physical signs of such a union.

Outwardly, then, Francis did not seem to be a happy man. But inwardly he was aflame with love for God and all God had created. That love is clearly reflected in the words of the canticle:

> *Most high, all-powerful, all good, Lord!*
> *All praise is yours, all glory, all honor*
> *And all blessing.*
> *To you, alone, Most High, do they belong.*
> *No mortal lips are worthy*
> *To pronounce your name.*
> *All praise be yours, my Lord, through all that you have made,*
> *And first my lord Brother Sun,*
> *Who brings the day; and light you give to us through him.*
> *How beautiful is he, how radiant in all his splendor!*
> *Of you, Most High, he bears the likeness.*
> *All praise be yours, my Lord, through Sister Moon and Stars;*
> *In the heavens you have made them, bright*
> *And precious and fair.*
> *All praise be yours, my Lord, through Brothers Wind and Air,*
> *And fair and stormy, all the weather's moods,*
> *By which you cherish all that you have made.*
> *All praise be yours, my Lord, through Sister Water,*
> *So useful, lowly, precious and pure.*
> *All praise be yours, my Lord, through Brother Fire,*
> *Through whom you brighten up the night.*
> *How beautiful is he, how gay! Full of power and strength.*
> *All praise be yours, my Lord, through Sister Earth, our*
> *   mother,*
> *Who feeds us in her sovereignty and produces*
> *Various fruits with colored flowers and herbs.*
> *All praise be yours, my Lord, through those who grant pardon*

For love of you; through those who endure
Sickness and trial.
Happy those who endure in peace,
By you, Most High, they will be crowned.
All praise be yours, my Lord, through Sister Death,
From whose embrace no mortal can escape.
Woe to those who die in mortal sin!
Happy those she finds doing your will!
The second death can do no harm to them.
Praise and bless my Lord, and give him thanks,
And serve him with great humility.

A Final Serenade

We began this chapter on Francis with the story of his late-night outburst of bell ringing and his rapturous joy in seeing the moon. Let us close with a story that illustrates the core of Francis's mystical relationship with his God. The episode was recorded by one of the brothers who unintentionally came upon Francis as he was expressing his overflowing joy to his Lord. Here's what the brother wrote:

> Sometimes Francis would act in the following way. When the sweetest melody of spirit would bubble up in him, he would give exterior expression to it in French, and the breath of the divine whisper which his ear perceived in secret would burst forth in French in a song of joy.
>
> At times, as we saw with our own eyes, he would pick up a stick from the ground and putting it over his left arm, would draw across it, as across a violin, a little bow bent by means of a string; and going through the motions of playing, he would sing in French about his Lord. This whole ecstasy of joy would often end in tears.

Like a lover who is so lost in the passion of love that he is oblivious to sadness or sorrow, Francis lived a life of such passionate devotion to God that all things—even the unpleasant things—were part of his hymn of praise to God.

Following in Francis's Footsteps

I know many people whose interest in Francis has led them to purchase a Francis bird feeder for their yards. This may sound simple, but something as basic as a bird feeder can help us call to mind

---

Living Free in a Culture of "Stuff"

Francis was part of the thirteenth-century mendicant movement that included Franciscans, Dominicans, Augustinians, and many others. *Mendicant* simply means "open handed" and refers primarily to new religious communities whose members approached God—and the entire world—as lowly beggars with open hearts and open hands.

Most European monks had worked at various moneymaking trades in their monasteries. These monks renounced personal property, owning property in common with other community members after the example found in Chapters Two and Four of the New Testament Book of Acts. But the new mendicant monks, usually called friars or brothers, owned nothing and depended on the goodwill of the faithful to whom they ministered.

Mendicants weren't freeloaders. They worked hard at trades or ministries, and in exchange for their labors they received enough food and clothing for one day and night. But they were prohibited from accepting money. Only when there was no work to be found did they rely on begging for their daily bread.

Begging was a radical concept in Francis's day, particularly since Europe was converting from the barter system to a means of exchange based on money. This transition paved the way for an unprecedented accumulation of wealth, growing disparities

Francis's love for the birds and for all creation. Some have even made their bird feeders the centerpiece of a prayer garden, where they can retreat for meditation and reflection in the morning or evening.

There are a million other ways to begin having more encounters with the natural world. Unfortunately, many of us spend our lives in sterile office buildings, in houses that are cut off from nature, or in cars that take us back and forth. Still, many office

between rich and poor, and new opportunities for exploitation. In this bullish context, Francis demonstrated that brothers could have peace and happiness without pursuing prosperity.

What relevance does the mendicant approach have to our own day and culture? I often begin my retreats at Little Portion Retreat and Training Center by asking people to "open their hands" to God. I do the same at my concerts.

I do this because in order for us to open our hands, we have to let go of anything that we are still clinging to. It is often the little things that we clutch covertly, thinking that no one will see. But God sees. Only when we let go of absolutely everything can God do whatever he wills in our life. Until then, we are trapped by the devices of our own making. We cannot get free.

Ironically, it's only when we become mendicants that we can receive the greatest treasure the world has ever known—the treasure of spiritual freedom, awakening, and rebirth. We receive this treasure when we let go of the old self, let the false person die, and allow ourselves to be born into a new life with Christ.

Have you become a mendicant for the Lord? Open your heart and hands to God. Then God can fill you with a whole new life of spiritual abundance beyond anything you ever dreamed possible before.

parks have walking trails employees can enjoy during their lunch breaks, and most of us live near a park or other outdoor area where we can reclaim and renew our connection to our Creator.

Francis also placed a premium on silence and solitude because he knew his mystical union with Christ depended on creating a good prayer environment. Though he was a loving and social man, Francis made sure he could enjoy extended periods of utter solitude with God. Do you set aside any times for silence and solitude in your life? For many of us such occasions don't come easily, but like other things in our lives, if we want to get them done we schedule them and write them down on our calendars or in our planners.

I encourage you to schedule some times of silence and solitude that allow you to begin developing a deeper relationship with God. You can do this on your own, taking a notebook, a spiritual book, or a Bible with you to a special place where you won't be disturbed. Or you may want to get some assistance from people at a local retreat center, monastery, or hermitage. Many such facilities offer programs and retreat days for those who seek a deeper and more joyful spiritual life.

There are so many other practical lessons we can learn from Francis. He was radical but he was also humble. Having come of age during the 1960s, I appreciate this unique combination. Many of us know how to tear things down, but Francis modeled a lifestyle of humility that built things up.

Francis was also able to embrace ancient traditions of desert spirituality but make these traditions new and vibrant for a contemporary culture. We need to find a way to achieve this kind of balance between old and new in our own lives.

I could mention many other things, but if I focus on what is central to Francis's spiritual life, I keep coming back to his love of his Father and his desire to spend all the time he could in his Father's loving presence.

LEARNING MORE ABOUT
Francis of Assisi

There's much in Francis's life that is worthy of deeper study and emulation. To learn more about Francis, you can read our earlier book, *The Lessons of St. Francis: How to Bring Simplicity and Spirituality into Your Daily Life* (Dutton/Plume, 1997/1998). Murray Bodo's *The Journey and the Dream* is an excellent brief book. And the mother of all Francis books is *St. Francis of Assisi: Omnibus of Sources of the Life of St. Francis.* This 1,665-page collection brings together the primary early biographies of the saint that were used in writing this chapter (Franciscan Herald Press).

The chapter mentions books on Franciscan mysticism by Maes and Lull, but one of the earliest and best volumes is St. Bonaventure's *Journey of the Soul into God* (available in the *Complete Works*, published by St. Anthony's Guild). You may also want to consult my book, *The Loved and the Beloved: A Way of Franciscan Prayer* (Crossroad, 1985).

There have been many movies about Francis's life, but Franco Zeffirelli's 1973 film, *Brother Sun, Sister Moon*, does the best job of capturing his life and portraying the joy he and his brothers and sisters shared. The soundtrack by Donovan may sound a bit dated today, but the rest of the movie has a beautiful, timeless quality that is both moving and inspiring.

My album *Troubadour of the Great King* (1988) is a musical celebration of all things Franciscan.

The Way of Suffering
Catherine of Siena

Giacomo Benicasa was a practical, hard-working man who made his living as a wool dyer in Siena's bustling textile market. His wife, Lapa, was a simple woman who was well acquainted with heart-break. She gave birth to twenty-five children, only twelve of whom survived infancy. All Lapa wanted for Catherine—her next-to-last child—was a normal childhood, an early marriage to a good husband, and a happy, predictable life.

But Catherine had other plans, none of them "normal" (for example, she lavished care on lepers and plague victims) or predictable (for example, after sensing God wanted her to live a more simple life, she began giving away her family's possessions). Her life was punctuated by a series of powerful supernatural encounters that left her caught midway between heaven and earth, and although few people would have called her happy, those who knew her most intimately said she possessed a profound joy.

Many Spanish mystics of the Middle Ages embraced an ascetic lifestyle of physical suffering and torturous self-discipline. But Catherine embraced this lifestyle more fanatically than any other mystic in this book, and her self-punishment left her body covered with gaping wounds, which she blithely referred to as her "flowers" and which undoubtedly contributed to her death in 1380 at the age of thirty-three.

Jesus died at thirty-three as well, and some say Catherine's early death was the fitting culmination of a life defined by an unusually close communion with Jesus. Walking home with her older brother one day, she looked across the Italian countryside to the massive cathedral of San Domenico. There in the sky was Jesus looking right back at her. He smiled gently into her eyes and blessed her with the sign of the cross.

Her brother couldn't figure out why Catherine had stopped dead in her tracks, and he tried to get her moving again by threatening that mother would be angry if they didn't return home soon. "If you could see what I see you would never try to disturb me," she told him.

A Homegrown Mystic

She didn't speak about her vision but began playing "nun," building little convents in the family garden and trying to instruct other neighborhood children in the ways of God. She also began spending hours alone praying to God and punishing her body by imitating the tortures she learned about from the often-gruesome legends of saints and martyrs. Raymond of Capua, who would later become her confessor and biographer, said such self-discipline was unusual in one so young. "The little disciple of Christ began to fight against the flesh before the flesh had begun to rebel."

Her mother began working overtime to point Catherine toward a normal childhood, but everything she attempted backfired. When she bought Catherine fancy clothes and tried to introduce her to prospective male suitors, Catherine shaved off her hair and hid in her room. When Lapa took her daughter to an upscale spa in hopes she would develop an appetite for the finer things in life, Catherine exposed herself to the hottest geothermal vents, scalding her skin as she meditated on the torments of hell. "She allowed herself not one mortal pleasure," writes Kathryn Harrison, author of a recent biography of the saint.

After Catherine refused to leave the house, Lapa came down hard, firing the household servants and forcing the frail Catherine to do all the cleaning, cooking, and sewing for a small army of family members, spouses, and textile workers. Catherine embraced this latest misfortune as she did the rest of life's problems, welcoming it as a blessing from God and determining to do the best she could.

If things hadn't changed, Catherine might have died anonymously, perhaps as she scrubbed a bathroom floor on her hands and knees. After all, most of the world's mystics have been unknown and unheralded. But once again, it was supernatural intervention that changed the course of her life. This time, Giacomo saw a dove hovering over Catherine's head as she attended to her household chores. Interpreting the dove as a sign of divine blessing, Giacomo relieved his daughter of her domestic tasks, allowed her to transform one of the house's small rooms into her own private monastic cell, and made Lapa promise to be more tolerant. Now Catherine was free to explore her unique mystical gifts more deeply.

The reclusive Catherine was overjoyed to have her own little room, which featured a simple crucifix hanging on the wall, a wooden table with an oil lamp that illumined the crucifix, and a couch, which she covered with wooden planks so it wouldn't be too comfortable.

Raymond of Capua would later write that Catherine's access to her own private room was less important than her access to God through an "inner cell" deep within her soul that was with her no matter where she was. "Now, having made herself an inner cell which no one could take away from her, she had no need ever to come out of it again," wrote Raymond.

Soon this little room became the regular meeting place for a small circle of disciples and priests who gathered for cozy but intense evenings of sharing that focused on times of prayer and conversations about the ways of God. Those talks and mystical encounters that Catherine experienced in her room would eventually propel her out into the larger world, where she would be hailed as a loving healer, a peacemaker between warring cities, a confidante of troubled popes—in other words, a key player in one of the darkest periods of Catholic history.

Catherine and Her Time

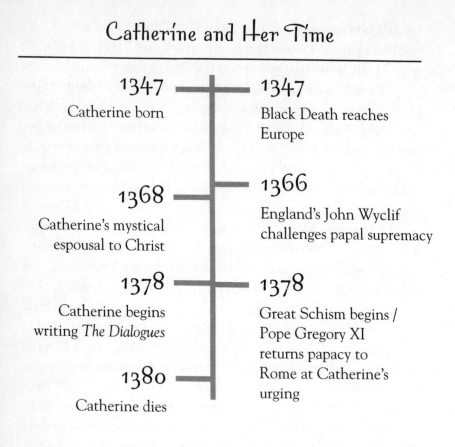

1347

Catherine born

1347

Black Death reaches
Europe

1368

Catherine's mystical
espousal to Christ

1366

England's John Wyclif
challenges papal supremacy

1378

Catherine begins
writing *The Dialogues*

1378

Great Schism begins /
Pope Gregory XI
returns papacy to
Rome at Catherine's
urging

1380

Catherine dies

"She was a mystic whose plunge into God plunged her deep into the affairs of society," wrote one scholar. Other writers have called Catherine a social mystic or a mystic activist.

She died in 1380 and was canonized by the church within a century. Then in 1970, at a time of growing calls for women's rights, she was named a Doctor of the Church, signifying that she was an eminent teacher of the faith. She was the first of only three women ever to receive this high honor (the others are Teresa of Avila and Thérèse of Lisieux, both of whom are discussed in later chapters of this book).

The other twenty-seven Doctors of the Church are men, and nearly all are well-educated theologians, ordained priests, or high-church officials. But not our simple Catherine, who would hear God speak these comforting words in her ear: "It is far better to walk by the spiritual counsel of a humble and unschooled person with a holy and upright conscience than by that of a well-read but proud scholar with great knowledge."

Catherine's saving grace was not her wisdom or learning but her intimate friendship with God. "She takes her rest then in me, the peaceful sea," says the voice of God in one of the many visions collected in Catherine's magnum opus, *The Dialogue*.

> When she feels the presence of my eternal Godhead she begins to shed sweet tears that are truly a milk that nourishes the soul in true patience. These tears are a fragrant ointment that sends forth a most delicate perfume.

An Inner Altar

Catherine's rich inner life generated numerous fascinating stories, many of which became a part of the official record of the church's investigation into whether or not she should be named a saint.

She was a member of the Dominican Third Order, which is today called secular. This meant she chose to live and worship in her home instead of in a monastery. She reports that she received her Dominican habit personally from St. Dominic, who had died a century before she was born. When she later donated the robe to a poor beggar, she said Christ himself had given her a new robe.

She also claimed that she received Holy Communion directly from Jesus, that she exchanged hearts with Christ, and that she received the stigmata (wounds of Christ) on her body. And near the end of her life, when she was too weak to walk forward to the communion rail in her local church, the bread and wine miraculously traveled to her.

But among her numerous mystical experiences, there were three events that shaped Catherine's soul and set the course for the rest of her life. One of these key events was her mystical death—a short period in which her body went cold while her heart was engulfed with a flaming love for God. As she explained to her confessor, "My soul was loosed from the body those four hours." From this time on, death and eternal union with Christ would be something that Catherine increasingly longed for.

A more joyous event was Catherine's spiritual marriage to Christ. News of the wedding came to her from Jesus during a vision that occurred when she was kneeling in prayer in her room:

> Since for love of me you have forsaken vanities and despised the pleasures of the flesh and fastened all the delights of your heart on me . . . I have determined to celebrate the wedding feast of your soul and to espouse you to me in faith.

The Virgin Mary performed the honors, placing Catherine's hand in the hand of Jesus and sealing the marriage with a brilliant ring that only Catherine could see. Many mystics might have been content with this, but Catherine was a hungry, restless soul who wanted to push on and explore new territory in her relationship with God.

Many mystics describe their desire for God as a burning fire, and that's how Catherine described her own spiritual passion in *The Dialogue*: "As a flame burns higher the more fuel is fed it, the fire in this soul grew so great that her body could not have contained it." Or as God tells her elsewhere in *The Dialogue*, "Once the soul has gained this ordinary light she ought not rest content. For as long as you are pilgrims in this life you are capable of growing and should grow."

The third key event in Catherine's mystical life happened one morning as she was conversing with Jesus in her room. He reminded her of the teaching he gave to a Jewish scholar in Matthew 22. Jesus had been challenged to name the greatest commandment in the Hebrew Scriptures, and his answer to the scholar came in two parts: "Love the Lord your God with all your heart and with all your soul and with all your mind," and "Love your neighbor as yourself."

Now Jesus spoke to Catherine about this all-important teaching. "I want you to fulfill both of these commandments," he said. "I want you to walk in the way with both your feet. I want you to fly to heaven on two wings."

Accepting the Call to Love

Like Moses, who responded to God's call by declaring himself unworthy of the assignment, Catherine initially pleaded incompetence when Jesus told her to love her neighbor. "I am but a woman and ignorant," she said. "What can I do?"

Jesus was reassuring. "Be brave and obedient when I send you out among people. Wherever you go I will not forsake you. I will be with you, as is my custom, and will guide you in all that you are to do."

Nothing could have been less inviting to the reclusive Catherine, who loved nothing more than to stay in her room and commune with God. Even brief encounters with her family members caused her discomfort. But Jesus had spoken. An order had been given. Now it was time for her to obey.

Without skipping a beat, Catherine offered her services at Santa Maria della Scala—the local hospital—and began caring for the sick and dying, including lepers and those who were suffering from a deadly outbreak of the plague. She asked to care for the worst cases, including the angriest and meanest patients and those who were closest to death's door. She knew she couldn't cure everyone's illnesses or prevent their deaths, but she could share their suffering, care for and pray for them, and try to administer to them some of the gracious gifts of divine love she herself had received. She also cared for Siena's poor by baking them bread.

As her reputation for sanctity and service grew, she was called in to serve as a mediator between feuding families and warring

Italian city-states. She also helped broker a peace agreement between the city of Florence and the government of the papal states. Such occasions gave Catherine the opportunity to serve as a peacemaker, and she felt that the times when she served as a bridge between fighting factions enabled her to live out the heart of the Gospel story, based as it was on Christ's call to heal the ancient rift between God and humanity.

Catherine's biggest assignment was healing the rift in the church caused by papal politics (see sidebar). Her encouragement helped Pope Gregory XI end the "Babylonian Captivity," but she was less successful at ending the resulting Great Schism, which was caused by rival "popes."

But regardless of the outcomes of her various campaigns, Catherine was faithful to the command of Jesus, and her experiences "in the world" helped deepen her faith. "Your neighbors," said the voice of God in *The Dialogue*, "are the channel through which all your virtues are tested and come to birth."

Talking to God

Catherine's public service did not end her times of communion with God. If anything, her prayer life deepened as she grew older and more mature. Two years before her death, the thirty-one-year-old Catherine began composing a document she called "my book." The resulting work, titled *The Dialogue*, is now hailed a classic of Western spirituality. She lays out the purpose of the book in the prologue:

> A soul rises up, restless with tremendous desire for God's honor and the salvation of souls. She has for some time exercised herself in virtue and has become accustomed to dwelling in the cell of self-knowledge in order to know better God's goodness toward her, since upon knowledge follows love. And loving, she seeks to pursue truth and clothe herself in it.

In order to better understand the truth, she asks God a series of questions concerning three major topics: herself, the reform of the church, and the state of the world. She also seeks God's advice on a "certain case" connected to her service in the world, but God only knows the specifics of this case.

Over the course of nearly 350 pages, God (who refers to himself as First Truth, Gentle Truth, Supreme Truth, and Exaltedness) responds to Catherine's inquiries. For anyone who has ever wanted to sit down and have a chat with God, the resulting book provides fascinating insights into Christian faith.

One of the recurring themes of *The Dialogue* is God's deep love for humanity. "I loved you before you came into being," God tells Catherine at one point. Elsewhere, he explains that his love for us found its perfect expression in the incarnation because we were too hard-hearted to receive his love in any other way. Humans, says God, "have, with the hand of free choice, encrusted their heart in a diamond rock that can never be shattered except by blood."

When it comes to human religiosity, God is impatient with spirituality that does not translate into tangible redemptive actions. "I want few words but many works," God says.

The most important and longest section of *The Dialogue* is titled "The Bridge." Here God helps Catherine understand the many ways his redemptive love permeates our world. Returning to the incarnation, God says, "I made of that cross an anvil where this child of humankind could be hammered into an instrument to release humankind from death and restore it to the life of grace." But sending Jesus to earth is just one facet of God's many labors on our behalf. "If I had taken back my love and ceased to love your being, you would not exist."

The reader can almost feel God's sorrow as he bemoans the sad state into which sinful humans have fallen. "They become unbearable to themselves," he says. "They who wanted to rule the world find themselves ruled by nothingness, that is, by sin." After detailing some of humanity's most depressing failures, God expresses his frustration: "O brutish souls! What have you done with your dignity?"

But God treasures the chances he has to commune with souls who are truly dedicated to him. "I am not a respecter of persons or status but of holy desires," he says, adding, "Everything you do can be a prayer."

God also wants Catherine to realize that times of trouble and testing don't mean he doesn't love her. "I send people troubles in this world so that they may know that their goal is not this life, and that these things are imperfect and passing," God says. "I am their goal, and I want them to want me." And those who persevere in times of trial will be the ultimate victors. "They can stand in the water of great troubles and temptations, but it cannot hurt them because they are anchored to the vine of burning desire. They find joy in everything."

Throughout *The Dialogue*, Catherine limits her comments to an occasional question or segue between topics. But on more than one occasion, she can't contain her overflowing joy. She exults,

> O eternal Father! O fiery abyss of charity! O eternal beauty, O eternal wisdom, O eternal goodness, O eternal mercy! O hope and refuge of sinners! O immeasurable generosity! O eternal, infinite Good! O mad lover! . . . Finite language cannot express the emotion of the soul who longs for you infinitely.

Beating Out the Devil

Nearly all of the mystics in this book believed that some form of rigorous self-discipline and self-denial was a prerequisite to holy living and possible communion with God. But in Catherine's case, this belief was taken to shocking and sometimes life-threatening extremes. Before we conclude our brief discussion of Catherine, it would be wise of us to examine her penitential practices, which have been a source of much controversy.

It is nearly impossible for us who live in the twenty-first century—a time of unprecedented wealth, technological development, and personal comfort—to get inside the heads of medieval mystics like Catherine, who equated physical comfort with spiritual corruption. Today, many Western societies confront epidemics of obesity. In Catherine's day, people battled the plague, and many Christians subscribed to the view that emaciated bodies typically housed holy souls.

The roots of this issue extend deep into human culture and belief, reaching back to the philosopher Plato, who argued that there was an impassible divide between two worlds: an idealized world of pure, changeless Forms and the so-called "real" world, which is subject to change, decay, and misunderstanding. Christians wrestled with this Platonic dualism in the centuries after Christ, ultimately declaring that Jesus was both God and man, flesh and spirit, ideal and real. But still, many monks and mystics who followed the lead of the most severe Desert Fathers taught that human flesh is inherently sinful and that salvation demands that we crucify our flesh.

Catherine grew up at a time when saintliness was equated with harsh ascetic practices, but she clearly took the idea of crucifying the flesh to a whole new level. She fasted; she denied herself sleep (allowing herself only one-half hour of sleep every other day, according to one account); she wrapped a chain with crosses around her body so tightly that it caused her to bleed, and she scourged her body three times a day with a chain that was tipped with sharp hooks. Although some of these practices were common among medieval monks and nuns, Catherine took them farther than most people, denying herself nearly all food and, near the end of her life, refusing to drink water or any other liquid but communion wine. This regimen left her weak and frail and subjected her to pain throughout her brief life.

Writer Rudolph Bell researched saints like Catherine to write his 1985 book, *Holy Anorexia*. Bell argued that many devout women of the Middle Ages suffered from a disease he called holy anorexia. Unlike contemporary eating disorders, which afflict women who are consumed with idealized notions of feminine beauty and sexiness, holy anorexia afflicted women who prized idealized notions of feminine godliness. Bell further argued that women like Catherine, who were spiritual loners, developed more extreme symptoms of the disease than women who lived in monasteries or abbeys, where others might modify their compulsions.

Anne Baldwin, author of a 1987 biography of Catherine, summarized some of the debate that swirls around the saint's private deprivations. "Catherine's life followed the model of the holy Dominican loner," she writes. "She sought heroic holiness. . . . Her fasting and self-denial went unchecked, developed into anorexia, and brought about her eventual death by starvation."

Some contemporary scholars argue that mystical experiences are nothing more than a biological byproduct of metabolism and blood chemistry. As this thinking goes, people who deny themselves proper nutrition cause the body to malfunction and the brain to misfire, resulting in visual and auditory hallucinations that seem so vivid and lifelike they are deemed supernatural visions.

But Baldwin and others articulate a more nuanced approach. Although they acknowledge that Catherine and other holy women may have been anorexic, they believe biology can never explain everything there is to understand about these saints. "The evidence seems to indicate that [Catherine] was both anorexic and holy," writes Baldwin. "Like many saints before her and after her she had a fatal disease. . . . But the disease never caused her to abandon God; nor did it cause Him to abandon her."

Settling this complicated debate about physical mortification is beyond the scope of this brief chapter. But those who want to follow in the footsteps of the mystics should be forewarned that potential dangers lie in their path if they choose a life that combines solitary devotion with harsh discipline.

Building Our "Inner" and "Outer" Lives

Catherine is a controversial saint. Some see her as a model for feminine holiness. Others see her as a symbol for harmful and unhealthy forms of devotion. Perhaps like most people, I see both good and worrisome things in the life of this unique Italian saint.

First, I believe Catherine's life is an endorsement of communal life. From the time of the Desert Fathers, God has called some people to be hermits. But I believe he has called far more people to live out their spiritual lives in the context of a committed and caring Christian community. For me and Brothers and Sisters of Charity at Little Portion Heritage community in Arkansas, that conviction has led us to join together, pooling our lives and our resources in ways that are counter to today's prevailing culture of individualism.

Others will find community in home groups or cell groups that are a part of their church or in long-term study groups that devote themselves to applying the Bible or spiritual books to their lives. The forms of Christian community are many and varied, but the important thing is that we all find a community that we can become a part of. The experience will not only help us grow, but we can help others with whom we come into contact.

At the same time, it is important for us to follow the example of Catherine by creating an "inner cell" deep within our souls that provides us with a sense of distance from the world and allows us to develop the mystical and contemplative dimensions of our spiritual lives. Some mystics spend a lifetime in a monastic cell, but those of us who live in the world need to build a similar house of prayer and devotion in our souls.

And regardless of where you live or what you feel your calling is, there is profound wisdom in Catherine's willingness to obey Jesus' command to love both God and her neighbor, no matter where that command led her. As Jesus told her in *The Dialogue*, "I want you to fulfill both of these commandments." Jesus is saying the same thing to us today: "I want you to walk in the way with both your feet. I want you to fly to heaven on two wings."

Sins of the Fathers

The New Testament speaks of the church as the mystical Body of Christ, but in Catherine's day the church was far from spotless. Or, as she put it in numerous writings, the church is infected with a moral decadence that's every bit as deadly as the disease of leprosy.

Many of the problems began at the top. In 1309, Pope Clement V moved the papacy from Rome to Avignon, France, because conditions weren't safe in Rome. The move, which historians call the Babylonian Captivity, separated the Pope from many of his followers and drastically increased the costs of operating the church. Then in 1378, Pope Gregory XI moved the papacy back to Rome at the urging of Catherine. But a rival group stayed behind in Avignon and competed with Rome for the title to papal authority. Historians refer to this split, which lasted until 1417, as the Great Schism.

Unfortunately, the problems with the church didn't end with the papacy but were spread throughout the institution. Devoted Catholics like Catherine were heartbroken and frustrated by the problems in their church, but Catherine did something others didn't do. She asked God for his perspective on the problems and recorded his comments in "The Mystical Body of Holy Church"— a lengthy chapter of her major book, *The Dialogue*. The exchange makes the sexual sins and financial misdeeds of twentieth-century priests, pastors, and televangelists look like child's play.

The ministers who serve as God's shepherds over the church have become "filthy beasts," according to God. "In every way you have become worse than the devil!" The problems surrounding the church's priests were almost too numerous to list. Their holy calling demands purity, but they are overcome with an all-too-human pride, a hankering after power and prestige, and a lust for money and riches. Church offices are sold to the highest bidders, and priests are so snared in sinful living that they hesitate to challenge those in their care to live holy lives. "They do not correct people for fear of losing their rank and position and their material possessions."

In one powerful passage, God says his priests are "bloated with pride." He added, "They never have their fill of gobbling up earthly riches and the pleasures of the world, while they are stingy, greedy, and avaricious toward the poor." Pride and selfishness have replaced love and compassion [and]

> the priests have abandoned the care of souls and given themselves over completely to guarding and caring for their temporal possessions. They leave behind my little sheep. . . . They go about fancily dressed, not like clerics and religious but like lords or court lackeys. . . . Their whole desire is feasting, making a god of their bellies.

Some priests even spend church funds on prostitutes. "They devour the souls who were bought with Christ's blood, eating them up in so many wretched ways." Others father children with women in the church.

> They have made themselves the devil's temple . . . these incarnate devils use the Church's property to adorn the she-devils with whom they live in sin and indecency. . . . After spending the night bedded down with deadly sin they go to celebrate [mass]! O tabernacles of the devil!

God can clearly see how bad things have become. "The stench reaches even up to me, supreme Purity," he says. But he doesn't tell Catherine to abandon the church. Rather, he tells her to honor the office of the priesthood and respect the sacraments that even sinful priests bestow.

> I have told you, dearest daughter, something of the reverence that ought to be given my anointed ones no matter how sinful they may be. . . . The sacramental mystery cannot be lessened or divided by their sinfulness.

God also tells Catherine that he will judge sinful priests more harshly and punish them more severely than other sinners, but he instructs her to continue praying and crying for his sin-infected Body. It's an assignment Catherine gladly welcomes. "I beg of you, let my eyes never rest, but in your grace make of them two rivers for the water that flows from you, the sea of peace."

LEARNING MORE ABOUT
Catherine of Siena

At the risk of sounding like a broken record, I recommend the version of Catherine's *The Dialogue* published by Paulist Press in its Classics of Western Spirituality series.

Catherine's life has been explored in numerous biographies. Anne B. Baldwin's *Catherine of Siena: A Biography* (Our Sunday Visitor, 1987), provides the traditional view.

Kathryn Harrison is one seventeen writers who contributed chapters to Paul Elie's book, *A Tremor of Bliss: Contemporary Writers on the Saints* (Harcourt, 1994). Although Harrison's chapter, "Catherine Means Pure," seems so self-absorbed that it tells us more about Harrison than it does Catherine, she has some interesting perspectives. And overall, Elie's book contains some fascinating insights into how modern thinkers are appropriating centuries of legend that has built up around the saints.

And if you're ever in Siena, make sure you visit Santa Maria della Scala, the hospital where Catherine worked. The facility is currently undergoing an extensive renovation, enabling contemporary visitors to see some of the glorious mosaics that decorated the walls in Catherine's day. (For information see "Some E. R.! Siena Led the Way" in the *New York Times*, Dec. 2, 2003.)

The Way of Service
Ignatius of Loyola

With its backdrop of courtly wealth and international adventure, its scenes of battlefield bravery and private despair, and its themes of spiritual transformation and ultimate triumph, the life story of the Spanish saint, Ignatius of Loyola, seems custom-made for a major Hollywood movie, perhaps starring Tom Cruise or Russell Crowe.

But as exciting as his life was, Ignatius is better known today for two creations that are far more influential now than they were at the time of his death nearly 450 years ago.

The first was a humble book titled *The Spiritual Exercises*, or the *Exercises*. Today, this simple but insightful book serves as a guide to spiritual enlightenment for tens of thousands of people around the world who participate in Ignatian retreats every year. Written by Ignatius and based on the life-changing lessons he had learned during his own difficult spiritual pilgrimage, *Exercises* balances mystical depth with commonsense practicality in ways that guarantee its continuing status as a Christian classic.

His second major creation was the Society of Jesus (also known as the Jesuits)—the religious order he founded to translate his deep spiritual passions into concrete action in the world. Today, nearly 25,000 Jesuits are engaged in teaching and preaching and serving in all regions of the earth.

The man behind these two lasting creations was the first of three important Spanish mystics who had a profound impact on matters of faith and practice around the time of the Protestant Reformation.

Born the year before Christopher Columbus sailed for the New World, Ignatius came of age at a time when Spain was emerging as the world's undisputed superpower. He could have easily spent his life as a member in good standing of the Spanish court, like some of his relatives. Or, like one of his brothers, he could have died as a globetrotting conquistador defending the honor of the throne.

But Ignatius had other battles to fight, many of them intense inner struggles against the demons of arrogance, pride, power, and pleasure, to which he devoted the early years of his life. In the end, this brave and crusty ex-soldier found solace in surrendering everything that meant the most to him for something that was both more elusive and more real. That's why I called the song I wrote about him "Surrender":

> *Take all my freedom*
> *My liberty, my will*
> *All that I have*
> *You've given to me*
> *So I offer it up to you*
> *I surrender all to Jesus*
> *I surrender it all to God's will*
> *I surrender it all for the Kingdom of God*
> *I surrender my life, my all*
> *Your grace and your love*
> *Are wealth enough for me*
> *Grant me these Lord Jesus*
> *And I'll ask for nothing more*
> *I surrender all to Jesus*
> *I surrender it all to God's will*
> *I surrender it all for the Kingdom of God*
> *I surrender my life, my all*

From Courtier to Beggar

Born in his family's sturdy castle, which was located in the Basque region of northern Spain, Ignatius was immediately thrust into a world of wealth, entitlement, and power. "The life of the Loyolas was a rich amalgam of deep religious tradition, sincere piety, burning passion and lust, fierce pride, and an attitude of aristocracy and nobility," writes W. W. Meissner in his insightful biography, *Ignatius of Loyola: The Psychology of a Saint*.

His mother died shortly after his birth, so Ignatius was put in the care of a nurse. He received a good education that included healthy doses of Catholic Christianity and romantic chivalry. And he was trained in all the skills and manners that were necessary for his success as a servant at the court of King Ferdinand of Castile, to whom the Loyola family had much earlier sworn its allegiance.

In due time, Ignatius learned how to handle a sword and to survive the many intrigues and power struggles that were a regular part of courtly life. He also learned to dress, dance, duel, gamble, and flirt like a courtier. Successful flirting required one to conduct romantic affairs without getting caught or killed, and as he admitted in his own autobiography, he was "fairly free in the love of women."

There was one particular woman Ignatius found more attractive than most. Although she was not identified in his autobiography, historians believe she may have been Dona Catalina, the sister of Emperor Charles V and the future queen of Spain. Ignatius, who wrote his autobiography in the third person, spent hour after hour "fancying what he would have to do in the service of a certain lady, of the means he would take to reach the country where she was living, of the verses, the promises he would make to her, the deeds of gallantry he would do in her service."

Such romantic fantasies were fun while they lasted, even if they were superficial and unfulfilling. Ignatius would later express his disgust with this period of his life. "Up to his twenty-sixth year he

Ignatius and His Time

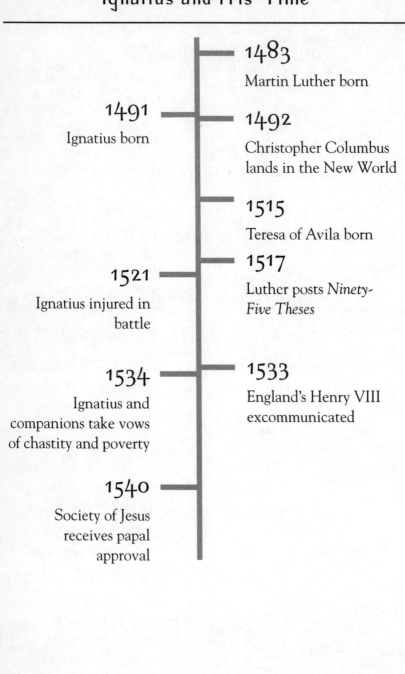

1483
Martin Luther born

1491
Ignatius born

1492
Christopher Columbus
lands in the New World

1515
Teresa of Avila born

1517
Luther posts *Ninety-
Five Theses*

1521
Ignatius injured in
battle

1534
Ignatius and
companions take vows
of chastity and poverty

1533
England's Henry VIII
excommunicated

1540
Society of Jesus
receives papal
approval

was a man given over to the vanities of the world," he wrote, "and took special delight in the exercise of arms, with a great and vain desire of winning glory."

Ignatius's idealized notions of gallantry were put to the test by the realities of war. It was May 1521, and a large French contingent of some three hundred men was attacking the town of Pamplona. Ignatius enlisted in the effort to defend the town. It was a tough battle, and the Spanish forces were badly outnumbered. Still, he held his ground, squaring off against the enemy as some of his disheartened comrades turned and fled for their lives.

But he paid for his bravery. A slug of metal fired by French artillery landed where he stood, wounding his left leg and completely shattering his right. Having been bundled up and taken to his family's castle for a long and painful recovery, Ignatius lay in his bed and fought off fever and illness. Thinking some light reading might help him pass the time, he requested a few volumes extolling the virtues of chivalry and the courage of soldiers. But the only books to be found in the castle's humble library were a lengthy history of the life of Christ and a collection of stories about the lives of the saints.

He reluctantly began reading these religious books, but soon the stories of holiness and godly service inflamed his imagination. Like Francis of Assisi, Ignatius's difficult period of postwar recovery turned into a powerful time of spiritual transformation. Here's how he described it:

> As he read the books over many times, he became rather fond of what he found written there. Putting his reading aside, he sometimes stopped to think about the things he had read and at other times about the things of the world that he used to think about. . . . Our Lord assisted him . . . [and] while reading the life of Our Lord and of the saints he stopped to think, reasoning within himself, "What if I should do what St. Francis did, what St. Dominic did?" So he pondered over many things that he found to be good, always

proposing to himself what was difficult and serious, and as he proposed them, they seemed to him easy to accomplish.

Ignatius also experienced the first of many mystical visions that would guide him throughout the rest of his life.

> One night, as he lay awake, he saw clearly the likeness of our Lady with the Holy Child Jesus, at the sight of which he received most abundant consolation for a considerable interval of time. He felt so great a disgust with his past life, especially with its offenses of the flesh, that he thought all such images which had formerly occupied his mind were wiped out.

Talk is cheap, and there are times when people's grand claims of inner conversion fail to be matched by significant outward change. But in the case of Ignatius, his conversion experience totally transformed his outlook and his behavior.

As his recovery progressed, he was determined to become a Christian pilgrim, setting his sights on visiting the holy city of Jerusalem. But sometimes our plans are interrupted by God's greater designs. And that's precisely what was about to happen to Ignatius.

Waiting for God

In order to reach Jerusalem, Ignatius had to go through Barcelona. And in order to reach Barcelona, he had to pass through Manressa—a small town where he planned to stay no more than a few nights. But those few nights turned into nearly a year, and the transformation he underwent in Manressa changed both the direction of his life and the course of later centuries of church history.

Embracing Francis as his role model and the rules of the Secular Franciscan Order (also known as the lay or Third Order) as his guide, Ignatius took residence in a cave outside of town where he practiced severe penances for his past sins. He fasted. He prayed. He scourged himself. He begged for morsels of food in the streets.

But donations were few, in part because he looked so dirty and bedraggled that people were scared to be near him, let alone hand him any food. This aspect of the life of Ignatius has always inspired me, perhaps because I lived as a secular Franciscan hermit in the early days of my own conversion as a Catholic Christian and later founded a new community based on Franciscan principles.

Over time, Ignatius aggressively turned his back on each and every facet of his former life. The man who had devoted most of his life to ascending the ladder of power and prestige began practicing a radical form of downward mobility. The man who had once clothed himself in fashionable finery wore beggars' rags and let his hair, fingernails, and toenails grow wildly out of control.

Soon people were calling him "Old Sack Man," but he was not bothered by their taunts. As he would write later, "If the soul chance to be inordinately attached or inclined to anything, it is very proper that it rouse itself by the exertion of all its powers to desire the opposite of that to which it was wrongly attached."

Meanwhile, Ignatius's soul was being flooded by mystical experiences that provided him such a deep and satisfying joy that he hardly noticed the pains and privations he endured. "At this time God treated him just as a schoolmaster treats a little boy when he teaches him," he wrote.

> As he sat, the eyes of his understanding began to open. He beheld no vision, but he saw and understood many things, spiritual as well as those concerning faith and learning. This took place with so great an illumination that these things appeared to be something altogether new.

At the same time, Ignatius began studying the Bible, books about the saints, manuals of devotion, and any other Christian literature he could put his hands on. But the more he studied, the more he began to feel torn between his spiritual passions, which he expressed through his penitential practices, and his passion for knowledge, which he had formerly associated with the worldliness of his courtly upbringing. We can be thankful that he ultimately decided he would need to receive a formal education.

This is an interesting crossroads in Ignatius's life, because as a mystic he felt he was learning much about God. But he knew that if he wanted to have any real impact on the world, he would need a decent education. And for Ignatius, having an impact on others was more important than his own personal fulfillment. This is a central characteristic of his mysticism of service.

His search for knowledge led him to some of the top universities of his day in Barcelona, Alcala, Salamanca, and Paris. And even though he was nearly three times the age of many fellow students, Ignatius applied himself with the zeal of a youth. For a time, he continued his harsh ascetical practices, but this led to conflicts with his studies.

> When he began to learn by heart, as has to be done in the beginning of grammar, he received new lights on spiritual things and new delights. So strong were these delights that he could memorize nothing nor could he get rid of them however much he tried.

No doubt, some of us would prize spiritual enlightenment over preparation for service to others. But Ignatius's call to serve was so strong that he curtailed his fasting and penances, spent fewer hours in mystical union with God, and devoted more of his time to his lessons.

When he wasn't praying or studying, Ignatius was most likely preaching to fellow students or local residents. None of his impromptu sermons survive, but those who heard him said his sermons were powerful and persuasive. Men fell to their knees and gave their lives to Jesus. Women swooned and fainted at his feet. Sinners cried out in despair. And prostitutes gave up the life they had led to follow Jesus.

In time, Ignatius's unconventional tactics aroused concerns among members of the Spanish Inquisition—a hard-nosed group that sought out and punished "heretics," focusing most of its energies on punishing those who promoted Europe's emerging Protestant Reformation. Time and time again, Ignatius had to defend himself against charges that he was an enemy of the church. His defenses didn't always succeed, and he was repeatedly jailed and commanded to cease his public preaching. At such times, he held his tongue and focused all his energies on acts of compassionate service.

He persevered, eventually winning over most of his harshest critics and attracting a loyal band of disciples who began to follow him around and preach with him. When people asked who they were, these brothers responded that they were "the company of Jesus." In time, this motley company of itinerant evangelists would become known as the Society of Jesus, receiving full papal approval in 1540.

During the final fifteen years of his life, Ignatius devoted most of his energies to overseeing the rapidly expanding work of the Jesuits. These duties brought him fame and might have led to his being elected pope if he had allowed others to lobby on his behalf. But Ignatius loved caring for souls more than he did administering an organization. So throughout his years with the Jesuits, he continued working on the book that would help make him one of history's best-known spiritual teachers.

Four Steps to Godliness

Though he was a man of action, Ignatius also understood the power of words, ideas, and literature. He had seen how ideals like chivalry could shape an entire culture and inspire people's devotion. He also knew the pivotal role Christian books had played in his own conversion.

One of his favorite books was *Imitation of Christ*, which he reportedly had memorized by the end of his life. Written by Augustinian mystic Thomas à Kempis in the late fifteenth century, *Imitation* has been called the most widely read religious book in the world, after the Bible. Such a claim is difficult to substantiate, but one thing is clear: no book had a more profound influence on the mystics featured in the book you are reading than *Imitation of Christ*.

Ignatius was the kind of student who learned best with a pen in his hand. He filled dozens of notebooks with some of the ideas he had come across in books, devoting most of his notes to strategies and methods he could use to teach people how to develop a deeper Christian experience. "Whatever he found useful for his own spiritual life, he wrote down in the hope that it might also be useful to others," says Anthony Mottola, whose 1964 translation of *The Spiritual Exercises* remains one of the most accessible versions.

Some of Ignatius's scribblings formed the basis of *The Spiritual Exercises*—a detailed manual on the spiritual life that he began writing about in 1521 and continued expanding and revising for the next quarter century. The book is based on two simple assumptions: (1) there are universal principles governing how well or how poorly a Christian progresses in the faith, and (2) these principles can be the basis of a step-by-step plan for spiritual growth that, if followed properly, virtually guarantees a measure of success. Or, as Ignatius put it in the book's introduction,

> Just as strolling, walking, and running are bodily exercises, so spiritual exercises are methods of preparing and disposing the soul to free itself of all inordinate attachments, and after accomplishing this, of seeking and discovering the Divine Will regarding the disposition of one's life, thus insuring the salvation of his soul.

Ignatius realized centuries ago how helpful a good spiritual manual could be, but as a wise teacher and devoted mystic, he had grander goals in mind than merely relaying facts and information. "It is not an abundance of knowledge that fills and satisfies the soul but rather an interior understanding and savoring of things," he wrote.

So this intrepid Spanish saint whom Mottola described as "a man of few ideas, but of immense practical genius" poured all his energies into writing his spiritual masterpiece. He used his analytical mind, his mystical heart, his soldier's discipline, and his intuitive understanding of human psychology to create a book that still changes lives today. Biographer W. W. Meissner called *Exercises* "one of the most influential works in Western civilization."

Typically, *Exercises* is used by groups of students participating in a four-week retreat led by a priest, pastor, or retreat leader. Ignatius addresses these teachers directly, commanding them to let God have his way in people's souls rather than force students into a mold of the teachers' making:

> It is much better and more fitting in seeking the Divine Will, that our Lord and Savior should communicate Himself to the devout soul, inflaming it with His love and praise, and disposing it to the way in which it can best serve Him in the future. Thus, the one who gives the *Exercises* should not lean either to the one side or the other, but standing in the middle like the balance of a scale, he should allow the Creator to work directly with the creature, and the creature with its Creator and God.

Although I come from a Franciscan and monastic perspective, I would heartily recommend that you take the opportunity to participate in an Ignatian retreat. Such retreats are offered regularly throughout the world. But even if you can't do so, studying *Exercises* will offer you a blueprint for spiritual progress that is organized to lead you through four steps (in four weeks) to godliness: (1) purification of the soul, (2) greater knowledge and love, (3) passionate commitment to Christ, and (4) the resurrected life.

Week One: Purification of the Soul

"Man is created to praise, reverence, and serve God our Lord, and by this means to save his soul," writes Ignatius.

> All other things on the face of the earth are created for man to help him fulfill the end for which he is created. From this it follows that man is to use these things to the extent that they will help him to attain his end. Likewise, he must rid himself of them in so far as they prevent him from attaining it.

In order to help his students break the bonds that bind them to earthly things, Ignatius recommends self-examination of the conscience, with particular emphasis on the recollection of personal defects and sins. *Exercises* instructs the student to "beg for an ever increasing and intense sorrow and tears for my sins." He adds, "Let me see myself as a sore and an abscess from whence have come forth so many sins, so many evils, and the most vile poison."

Aware that mental exercises produce only limited results, Ignatius tries to involve the whole person by requiring students to meditate on mental images of Christ hanging on the cross and sinners suffering torments in hell. With such images firmly in mind, the student is to ask, "What have I done for Christ? What am I now doing for Christ? What ought I do for Christ?" And toward the end of Week One, Ignatius attempts to bring home this sense of alienation from God by closing the shutters and doors of his room and sitting in utter darkness. This is not some morbid preoccupation with sin and depravity but an honest appraisal of our current human condition. As is frequently said in the Christian tradition, humility means grasping the truth about reality, and the beginning of humility is an honest knowledge of ourselves.

The final purifying step is penance, which comes in three forms: abstaining from food, abstaining from sleep, and inflicting pain on one's own flesh. The goal, says Ignatius, is not that we wallow in despair and self-abuse but that we develop a frank appreciation for our own sinfulness and resolve to leave sin behind in order to plunge into a deeper communion with God.

Week Two: Greater Knowledge and Love

This lesson begins with an intriguing assignment. Students are asked to imagine that they are loyal subjects of a powerful king and to consider what forms of loyalty might reasonably be due such a sovereign ruler. Then the students are asked to consider the fact that they are servants of an Eternal King, before whom all humanity must humbly bow. This has a particularly Franciscan flavor, as Francis himself idealized spiritual knighthood and promoted the service of the heavenly kingdom on earth.

Whereas Week One focused on fostering regret for sin through the examination of the conscience, Week Two fosters love for God by meditating on his goodness. The goal "is to smell and taste in my imagination the infinite fragrance and sweetness of the Divinity," writes Ignatius.

"A Meditation on Two Standards" contrasts the kingdom of God with the realm of Satan—"the mortal enemy of our human nature." And "The Three Classes of Men" encourages students to be people who "act only as God our Lord shall inspire them," not to lust after some of the very things that were once Ignatius's chief preoccupations: "riches," "the empty honor of the world," and "unbounded pride."

One can hear the echoes of Ignatius's courtly upbringing in the sections on kingdoms in conflict and different classes of men. The activities in Week Two encourage students to make wise choices about what they will do with their lives. "For each one must realize that he will make progress in all spiritual matters in proportion to his flight from self-love, self-will, and self-interest."

Week Three: Passionate Commitment to Christ

Students meditate on the Passion of Christ while making a "serious effort to strive to grieve, to be sad, and lament." Many of us would rather focus on the joys of Easter than the sorrows of the Passion, but Ignatius believed appropriate reflection on Christ's brutal crucifixion would instill a deepened sense of thankfulness for his willingness to suffer for our sins, and a heightened sense of commitment to his service. This brief section concludes with guidelines for fasting, once again showing the importance of disciplining the flesh, as well as the soul and spirit in a complete and balanced approach to Christian spirituality.

Week Four: The Resurrected Life

Balancing practical and mystical concerns, this section opens with the "Contemplation to Attain Divine Love," which says, "Love ought to be manifested in deeds rather than words." The section closes with a lengthy summary of the Gospels titled "The Mysteries of the Life of Our Lord," which provides students with plenty of raw material for periods of contemplation and meditation. Between these two elements is a brief lecture on prayer that beautifully captures the concept of surrender that is at the core of Ignatius's spirituality and that inspired the song lyrics that I included near the beginning of this chapter:

Soldiers for God

Even after he turned his back on his courtly upbringing and military service, Ignatius of Loyola remained a charismatic man and natural leader who thought of himself as a soldier in the service of Christ. He readily attracted others to his cause and transformed an informal band of brothers into one of the most influential religious orders in the Catholic Church.

The origins of the Society of Jesus are in Paris, where Ignatius was a student from 1528 through 1535. While there, he met Francis Xavier and eight other students who pledged to live a life of poverty, serve the Pope however and wherever he commanded, and do whatever else was determined to be, in the words of the group's motto, "For the Greater Glory of God." The group's mission was to work for "the progress of souls in Christian life and doctrine and the propagation of the faith."

Against his will, Ignatius was elected the group's first superior in 1541, and running the group was his central preoccupation for the remaining fifteen years of his life. During that time, he wrote the society's constitution, helped spread its work around the globe, established many monastic houses and colleges throughout the world, and earned the respect of bishops, popes, and secular kings.

Take, O Lord, and receive all my liberty, my memory, my understanding, and my entire will, all that I have and all that I possess.
Thou has given all to me, to Thee O Lord, I return it. All is Thine;
dispose of it according to Thy will. Give me Thy love and Thy
grace, for this is enough for me.

Although no manual can guarantee immediate or universal
results, *The Spiritual Exercises* has been changing lives for centuries,
and tens of thousands of people say that doing the *Exercises* has
helped them experience a deeper relationship with God and find
more meaningful ways to serve Christ with their lives. "Few men in
the history of the world have touched the lives of their fellow men

---

There were a thousand Jesuits by the time of Ignatius's death.
Today, the order has nearly 25,000 members running schools, con-
ducting missionary activities, and overseeing other programs in
every region of the world. Xavier began his famous mission to India
in 1542, and Jesuits were also renowned for their work in India and
North America.

As he neared death, Ignatius described the characteristics
that any future superior of the order should possess. "The first is
that he should be closely united with God our Lord and intimate
with Him in prayer and all his actions." In addition, he should be
a good example to others, be "independent of all passions," "know
how to mingle rectitude and necessary severity with kindness and
gentleness," "possess magnanimity and fortitude of soul," "be
endowed with great understanding and judgment," and finally,
"he ought to be one of those who are most outstanding in every
virtue."

Like everyone, Ignatius had his shortcomings. But according
to those who knew him best, he exemplified each one of these
characteristics. Who wouldn't want to follow a spiritual leader
like this?

as profoundly and pervasively as Ignatius of Loyola," writes W. W. Meissner. And if we are willing to learn from this devoted saint and spiritual master, perhaps we can experience some of the mystical heights and practical influence he knew.

Exercise for Flabby Souls

Ignatius compared his *Spiritual Exercises* to activities like strolling, walking, and running. But it might be easier for us to understand what he means by comparing his program for spiritual growth to an hour-long workout at the local gym. Regardless of which illustration works best for you, the lesson is the same: spiritual laziness and moral flab can be as destructive to our souls as extra pounds are to our physical health.

Or, as Ignatius put it in *The Spiritual Exercises*, "The closer the soul approaches Him, the more it is disposed to receive graces and gifts from His divine and sovereign goodness."

Another important dimension of Ignatian spirituality is its emphasis on something called the "revelation of thoughts." The sacrament of confession focuses on seeking forgiveness for sins already committed, but the revelation of thoughts tries to head sin off at the pass by examining the soul and exposing its contents to a trusted spiritual director.

This kind of spiritual openness and vulnerability was a central feature of desert spirituality (see the second chapter) and has been a recurring feature of monastic life in many orders ever since. Interest in spiritual direction is growing again in our day, and many Protestant seminaries offer courses in this powerful ancient practice. At a time when so much spirituality is marked by a kind of hyper-individualism, disciplines like the revelation of thoughts can restore a sense of mutual accountability.

One final lesson that comes from examining the life of Ignatius is his willingness to surrender absolutely everything he had for something much better. He sacrificed the power and prestige that came with being a part of one of the world's leading powers to become a poor beggar, dependent only on the love and mercy of God. In time, God brought him prestige of a new kind, but this triumph would not have occurred without the surrender God required.

LEARNING MORE ABOUT
Ignatius of Loyola

Ignatius's *The Spiritual Exercises* has been continuously in print for more than four hundred years and is readily available in many translations and editions today. The edition we used here was Anthony Mottola's straightforward 1964 translation, published in paperback by Image/Doubleday.

There are many ways to learn more about this saint's amazing life. A brief but thorough biographical essay by acclaimed Catholic writer Ron Hansen can be found in Paul Elie's *A Tremor of Bliss: Contemporary Writers on the Saints* (Harcourt, 1994). A much more thorough study is W. W. Meissner's *Ignatius of Loyola: The Psychology of a Saint* (Yale, 1992). Meissner is a Jesuit and a professor of psychoanalysis at Boston College, and his four-hundred-page biography does a good job of explaining Ignatius to contemporary readers.

For a recent history of the Jesuits that provides a balanced account of both the order's stellar accomplishments and embarrassing missteps, read Jonathan Wright's *God's Soldiers: Adventure, Politics, Intrigue, and Power—A History of the Jesuits* (Doubleday, 2004).

Information on Ignatian retreats using *The Spiritual Exercises* can be found by calling your local Catholic diocese.

The song "Surrender" is from my 1990 album, *The Hiding Place*.

The Way of Union
Teresa of Avila

Gianlorenzo Bernini was an Italian sculptor and architect who practiced Ignatius's spiritual exercises and attempted to capture the inner dimensions of the human soul in his art. One of his most moving works is a sculpture housed in the Cornaro Chapel of Rome's Santa Maria della Vittoria Church.

There, in cold white marble that is polished to a brilliant sheen, Bernini has beautifully captured the fiery spirit of one of history's most beloved and influential mystics. *The Ecstasy of St. Teresa* shows the sixteenth-century Spanish mystic writhing. She is either in pain, in bliss, or in some overpowering combination of both. Her eyes are closed but her mouth is open, suggesting that her senses have been overcome by the sheer force of her experience.

Standing slightly above her is a smiling angel who holds a sharp-pointed spear. And falling down upon them from heaven above are dozens of brilliant white rays, symbolizing an overflowing of divine blessing. The sculpture is based on a supernatural experience Teresa describes in her autobiography:

> I would see beside me . . . an angel in bodily form. He was not tall, but short and very beautiful. In his hands I saw a long golden spear and at the end of the iron top I seemed to see a point of fire. With this he seemed to pierce my heart several times so that it penetrated to my entrails. When he drew it out, I thought he was drawing them out with it and he left me completely afire with great love of God. The pain was so sharp that it made me utter several moans; and so

excessive was the sweetness caused me by this intense pain that one can never wish to lose it, nor will one's soul be content with anything less than God.

Bernini's *The Ecstasy of St. Teresa* depicts in stone something that mystics like Teresa repeatedly struggled to convey in words— the experience of a soul caught up in ecstatic union with God. And she spent her final years trying to find the words to describe her many and varied spiritual experiences in the now-classic book, *Interior Castle*.

Her goal was to provide a blueprint for people seeking a deeper connection to God. But unlike many of today's best-selling self-help authors and speakers, she wasn't puffed up about her own abilities. She repeatedly expressed her own lack of spiritual qualifications and readily admitted her inability to convey what she meant.

"I am not meant to write," she confessed at one point. "I have neither the health nor the wits for it."

Bernini's powerful art conveys a depth of meaning that Teresa's simple words often fail to achieve, but his sculpture shows only one side of this multifaceted saint. *The Ecstasy of St. Teresa* shows a woman who is lost to the world, but she didn't spend her life in seclusion awaiting the next of her many raptures. She was a busy, no-nonsense woman who founded a monastic order called the Discalced (unshod) Carmelites. She established more than a dozen new convents, worked tirelessly to reform the church, and served as a spiritual adviser to princes and priests.

"She was an extremely businesslike mystic," writes biographer Cathleen Medwick. And writer Francine Prose sees flashes of humanity shining through Teresa's many superhuman experiences. "She is funny, edgy, self-mocking, and extremely sympathetic toward the excesses and self-dramatization that goes along with being young." Meanwhile, critics like Josef Breuer—a colleague of Sigmund Freud—sees her as all too human and far too irrational. Breuer derisively brands Teresa as "the patron saint of hysteria."

But perhaps Bernini understood Teresa best. He knew her ecstatic reveries were the glue that held her body and soul together through her many years of stress caused by organizational responsibilities, institutional conflict, and physical torment that resulted from recurring illness.

Balancing the Mystical and the Mundane

Born in 1515, Teresa entered the Carmelite Incarnation monastery in her hometown of Avila, Spain, when she was twenty years old. But none of her fellow sisters considered her to be particularly devout. Young women of that time had two basic choices in life: they could be wives or they could be nuns. Teresa chose the latter path, but it would take time for her to embrace her vocation.

She was walking to prayer one day when her eyes focused on a haunting image of the wounded Christ. Before she knew it, the image had touched her soul and unleashed "a great flood of tears." Soon thereafter, she experienced the first of many locutions. She was wrestling with questions about how God could love a sinful woman like her when a voice from deep within her commanded: "Do not look too deeply into this, but serve Me."

These developments would mark a major turning point in her life. She had once merely gone through the motions of the monastic life, but now she was focused on spending more time in prayer and fostering greater devotion. "All my conversation was with God," she later recalled.

In time, Teresa developed a desire to live a more disciplined and demanding life than was common in the Carmelite monasteries of her day. Her zeal won her the respect of her sisters, who elected her abbess of Incarnation. But she became convinced that a return to ancient disciplines of poverty and prayer could reform the Carmelites.

Teresa and Her Time

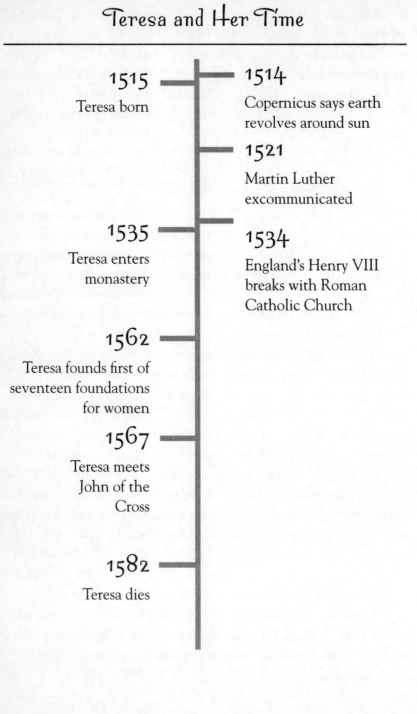

1515
Teresa born

1514
Copernicus says earth revolves around sun

1521
Martin Luther excommunicated

1535
Teresa enters monastery

1534
England's Henry VIII breaks with Roman Catholic Church

1562
Teresa founds first of seventeen foundations for women

1567
Teresa meets John of the Cross

1582
Teresa dies

Help came from two surprising sources. Jesus reportedly appeared to Teresa and ordered her to pursue her reform. And a devout young Carmelite mystic named John of the Cross (see the next chapter) partnered with Teresa in the work of renewal.

Beginning in 1562, Teresa founded a series of seventeen foundations for women, and with John's help she worked to reform the Carmelite men's houses. After her death, their reform movement would become a separate order—the Discalced Carmelites, whose shoeless feet were a powerful symbol of their commitment to a life of simplicity and contemplative prayer.

Biographer Cathleen Medwick says Teresa's take-charge approach to life flaunted the gender stereotypes of her day. "Though she was a woman and nun, she moved through the world with assurance, like a man." Unlike other women of her day, Teresa traveled throughout Spain and stayed at roadside inns, just like men. She ran the business affairs of her foundations and directed the spiritual lives of her sisters.

With her increasingly high profile came more attacks from male religious leaders, some of whom worried about her theology and some of whom were frankly jealous of her growing power and authority. She was repeatedly reported to the Spanish Inquisition, which investigated her writings, and was at least once accused of sexual immorality—a ludicrous charge that did little to slow her down.

Teresa lived a full and hectic life until her death in 1582, and the thing that most astounded those who knew her best was her knack for immersing herself in all manner of secular matters without losing her spiritual passion. There were many anecdotes indicating she seemed to be suspended between two worlds, including legends about how she would begin levitating during a chapter meeting or fall down faint from rapture during a communal meal.

But Teresa believed she could encounter God in the kitchen "among the pots and pans" as well as she could in the chapel. And she worked to maintain this delicate balancing act between the sublime and the mundane for the rest of her life.

Building a Mystical House

The European Renaissance of the fourteenth, fifteenth, and six-teenth centuries inspired a rebirth of learning that influenced such diverse disciplines as science, philosophy, theology, and architecture. A new emphasis on modern, rational methods prevailed in all fields, and there are signs that Teresa attempted to mimic such approaches when she came to write *Interior Castle*, which is widely hailed as her mystical masterpiece. She was much more critical of her literary achievement. "I have little to say that I have not already said in other books," she admits in the introduction.

Teresa had wanted to pass on her thoughts about prayer to her Carmelite sisters, and her own confessor had commanded her to do so. But living at a time of religious revolution made her cautious. The flinty-eyed censors from the Spanish Inquisition were searching for heresy in her *Vita*, or autobiography. Her other major spiritual treatise, *The Way of Perfection*, was not widely available. And she had already burned her only copy of her own *Meditations on the Song of Songs* after a concerned theologian thought it might be safest to do so.

So when Teresa finally sat down to compose her final book, she spoke less directly than she wanted to. She adopted the metaphor of a castle and concealed all references to her own experiences by cloaking them in the third person. And she grumbled about the project at nearly every step along the way:

> Few tasks which I have been commanded to undertake by obedi-ence have been so difficult as this present one of writing about mat-ters relating to prayer: for one reason, because I do not feel that the Lord has given me either the spirituality or the desire for it; for another, because I have been suffering from such noises and weak-ness in the head that I find it troublesome to write even about nec-essary business. But, as I know that strength arising from obedience has a way of simplifying things which seem impossible, my will very gladly resolves to attempt this task although the prospect seems to cause my physical nature great distress.

Over the course of the next few months, she was tempted to give up the project, but thoughts of her beloved sisters inspired her to keep at it. "It is they whom I shall be addressing in what I write," she says.

> It seems ridiculous to think that I can be of any use to anyone else. Our Lord will be granting me a great favor if a single one of these nuns should find that my words help her to praise Him ever so little better. His Majesty well knows that I have no hope of doing more.

We should be thankful that Teresa did continue writing down her thoughts on prayer and the mystical journey. By following her footsteps through the seven mansions of her *Interior Castle*, we can learn some of the secrets of the journey from a trusted pioneer who knows the territory.

First Mansions: God and Humanity

Teresa's ultimate destination in *Interior Castle* is the metaphorical seventh mansion, where the longing soul and loving Lord will be united in spiritual marriage to experience deep and lasting communion. But before setting out on her journey, she checks to make sure her readers have the necessary understanding of both human nature and the heart of God.

Human nature is a paradox. We are creatures of great beauty and dignity who are created in God's image. At the same time, we are sin-darkened beasts who resemble "malodorous worms." But thankfully, no soul is too dark for eternal love to illuminate.

"God's will is that no bounds should be set to his works," declares Teresa. "I can find nothing with which to compare the great beauty of a soul. The soul of the righteous man is nothing but a paradise, in which, as God tells us, He takes His delight."

Throughout her book and the works of other Christian mystics, one topic that frequently reappears is the question of why some people appear to receive greater blessings from God than others. Teresa is as mystified as anyone who wrestles with this question, but there's one thing she's certain about: mystical experiences are nothing to brag about. "If the Lord grants you these favors, it will be a great consolation to you to know that such things are possible; and, if you never receive any, you can still praise His great goodness."

Many writers have labored to describe the mystical journey, and some have failed miserably, becoming lost in ethereal language and abstract concepts that fail to connect with their readers or produce any lasting impact in their lives. But one of the central themes of *Interior Castle* is the close connection Teresa sees between the mystical and the practical.

"True perfection consists in the love of God and our neighbor," she writes, "and the more nearly perfect is our observance of these two commandments, the nearer to perfection we will be."

Second Mansions: Prayer and Penance

Those souls who want to make progress in the spiritual life must learn to distinguish the voice of God from the chaos and confusion that surrounds us. "These souls can understand the Lord when He calls them; for, as they gradually get nearer to the place where His majesty dwells, He becomes a very good Neighbor to them."

Some of us may become distracted by the cares of the world, but God continues seeking us out. "This Lord of ours is so anxious that we should desire Him and strive after His companionship that He calls us ceaselessly, time after time, to approach Him."

Prayer is the means by which the soul approaches God more closely. And for Teresa, effective prayer is straightforward, not overly adorned with flowery language or lots of thees and thous. "Do not think we have to use strange jargon or dabble in things of which we have no knowledge or understanding," she writes.

Rather, the heart of prayer is lowly submission. "All that the beginner in prayer has to do—and you must not forget this, for it is very important—is to labor and be resolute and prepare himself with all possible diligence to bring his will into conformity with the will of God."

For Teresa, spirituality isn't an escape from examining our sinful nature but an invitation to scrutinize our inner selves ever more closely. "It is absurd to think that we can enter Heaven without first entering our own souls, without getting to know ourselves, and reflecting upon the wretchedness of our nature."

Third Mansions: Love Beyond Reason

If Teresa's friend John of the Cross had written *Interior Castle*, it would be logical and orderly, just like *Dark Night of the Soul*. But Teresa was a raw and reluctant writer who sometimes veered wildly off course, surprising even herself with the directions her thoughts took.

"And now I forget what I was saying," she writes in one of many asides. "I have been indulging in a long digression. Whenever I think of myself I feel like a bird with a broken wing."

Sooner or later she always got back on track, and she returned to the topic of penance by confronting her own sins. "You would like to think I had been very holy, not this wretched and foolhardy woman."

Teresa believed that living and praying in community helped her see her own failings. "It is a great advantage for us to be able to consult someone who knows us, so that we may learn to know ourselves, [but] let us look at our own shortcomings and leave other people's alone."

Themes pop up like mechanical ducks in a shooting arcade, and Teresa took aim at each one before racing on to the next. Are mystical experiences proof of our spiritual maturity? No, they often show how immature we are. "We are fonder of spiritual sweetness than of crosses." Is faith more important than works? No, our actions demonstrate our faith. "Words are not enough," she says.

She also wanted us to pursue God with a lover's passionate desire rather than an accountant's calculated restraint. "They are eminently reasonable folk!" she writes. "Their love is not yet ardent enough to overwhelm their reason."

Fourth Mansions: The Prayer of Quiet

The closer we draw to God, the less solid guidance Teresa has to offer us. "There is no infallible rule about it," she says. "The Lord gives when He wills and as He wills and to whom He wills, and, as the gifts are His own, this is doing no injustice to anyone."

The mind is important, but it's the desires of the heart that propel us on. "Knowledge and learning are a great help in everything," she writes. Still, "the important thing is not to think much, but to love much; do, then, whatever most arouses you to love." The love Teresa speaks of is not a selfish sentimentalism but an unwavering submission that puts higher things first. "Love consists not in the extent of our happiness, but in the firmness of our determination to try to please God in everything."

Teresa used an illustration to introduce something she called the Prayer of Quiet: There are two fountains. One is filled by great labor, the water being transported over long distances by assorted man-made conduits. "The other has been constructed at the very source of water and fills without making any noise," she writes.

Our own prayer lives should resemble the second fountain. Instead of working up a spiritual fervor with our own efforts, we should plant ourselves where God is and effortlessly meditate on his heavenly delights. "When it is His Majesty's will and He is pleased to grant us some supernatural favor, its coming is accompanied by the greatest peace and quietness and sweetness within ourselves."

Fifth Mansions: Growing Union, Continuing Temptation

"Oh, the secrets of God!" cries out Teresa as she strains to describe times of communion with God that are so intimate and so sweet that she calls them "a delectable death." Ultimately, her words fail her.

> I think it would be better if I were to say nothing of the Mansions I have not yet treated, for no one can describe them, the under-

standing is unable to comprehend them and no comparisons will avail to explain them.

But Teresa had been commanded to explain these very things, so she soldiered on, making two major points. First, union with God is desirable, but there's little we can do to make it happen besides open our hearts: "Although this work is performed by the Lord, and we can do nothing to make His Majesty grant us this favor, we can do a great deal to prepare ourselves for it." One way to prepare ourselves is to offer the Prayer of Union, through which we lay down our own notions of godliness and await the Lord's visitation, whatever form it may take.

Second, as we draw closer to God the devil steps up his efforts to draw us away. "There is no enclosure so strictly guarded that he cannot enter it, and no desert so solitary that he cannot visit it," writes Teresa. Our only security is in absolute submission to God. "We must continually ask God in our prayers to keep us in His hand."

Over time, our hearts are more like wax which, when warmed, becomes increasingly pliable. "That soul has now delivered itself into His hands and His great love has so completely subdued it that it neither knows nor desires anything save that God shall do with it what He wills."

Sixth Mansions: Wounds of Love

The book's longest and most meandering section contains descriptions of spiritual rapture that sound like the blueprint for Bernini's marble sculpture: "The soul has been wounded with love for the Spouse and seeks more opportunity of being alone, trying so far as is possible . . . to renounce everything which can disturb it in this its solitude."

Raptures are more common in this mansion, as the soul "becomes consumed with desire" and yearns for nothing more than the loving pain that God brings. "Such a soul would gladly have a thousand lives so as to use them all for God, and it would like everything on earth to be tongue so that it might praise him."

The soul may experience moments of spiritual rapture, but the body continues to suffer assorted trials, torments, and tempests. "God gives no more than we can bear," promises Teresa, but even the strongest souls doubt. "The best medicine . . . for enabling the soul to endure it is to occupy oneself with external affairs and works of charity and to hope in God's mercy."

Seventh Mansions: Spiritual Marriage

Break out the champagne and cut the cake, for the lifelong pursuit of spiritual union with God has resulted in the ultimate consummation, flooding the soul with joy, tranquility, and the "deepest silence." The scales are removed from our eyes, enabling us to see more clearly the favors God grants us. Our souls, once dark, are now illumined by an inner light.

This union fills our hearts with joy while granting God a sacred haven where he can share his love. "He must needs have an abiding-place in the soul, just as He has one in Heaven, where His Majesty alone dwells," she writes. "So let us call this a second Heaven."

But even though the soul has experienced the union it has craved, this is not the end of the spiritual journey. "Love, I believe, can never be content to stay for long where it is," writes Teresa, content to let her Divine Lover continue leading her wherever he wills.

A Spirituality for Soccer Moms

Many of us want to be closer to God, but few among us have a few decades to spend in a monastery. Teresa was both a mystic and a very busy woman, and thanks to the nuggets of wisdom found in her life and teaching, all of us can gain insight into developing our relationship with God, whether we are a harried soccer mom, an overworked business manager, or just an average Joe who is trying to love God more deeply in the midst of a noisy and chaotic culture.

At times, I feel as though Teresa's writing is too detailed and methodical. She seems to work overtime to define the indefinable. At other times, she succeeds perhaps better than any other mystic in showing us how to balance the practical and the mystical, the pragmatic and the ecstatic, the demands of this world with the reality of the eternal realm.

And like many mystics, she draws at least some of her inspiration from a key passage in the New Testament. At the end of the tenth chapter of the gospel of Luke, Jesus visits the home of a woman named Martha. This was twenty centuries before a woman named Martha Stewart would transform tasks like housekeeping and decorating into the rituals of a new kind of domestic religion. But even way back then, the Martha who hosted Jesus wanted everything to be done just right for his visit. Meanwhile, her sister Mary paid little attention to such concerns. All Mary wanted to do was sit at Jesus' feet and drink in everything he had to say.

Martha was irked by Mary's lack of domestic responsibility and complained to Jesus: "Lord, don't you care that my sister has left me to do the work by myself? Tell her to help me!"

"Martha, Martha," Jesus answered. "You are worried and upset about many things, but only one thing is needed. Mary has chosen what is better, and it will not be taken away from her."

Millions of words have been written and preached about these five brief verses, with many mystics claiming Jesus favored the contemplative Mary over the duty-bound Martha. But as the ever-practical Teresa saw it, both sisters were expressing their love for Jesus. "Martha and Mary must work together when they offer the Lord lodging," she writes near the end of *Interior Castle*.

Mystics and activists were not spiritual opposites of Teresa. She saw contemplation and action as two sides of the same coin: both are means by which we can serve God and show him our love.

"Do you know when people really become spiritual?" she asks. "It is when they become the slaves of God and are branded with

His sign, which is the sign of the Cross, in token that they have given Him their freedom." And besides, says Teresa, *what* we do isn't half as important as *why* we do it. "The Lord does not look so much at the magnitude of anything we do as at the love with which we do it."

Such practical wisdom was a hallmark of Teresa's life and teaching. She criticized mystics who became lost in their own personal spiritual reveries and failed to have any significant impact on the

---

An Unusual Doctor

Writer Bert Ghezzi explored 365 heroes of the faith in his book, *The Voices of the Saints: A Year of Readings*. His description of Teresa's humanity and warmth helps explain why she is so popular with so many people today:

> A friend was once surprised to find St. Teresa gorging herself on a partridge. "What would people think?" asked the friend. "Let them think whatever they want," said Teresa. "There's a time for penance, and there's a time for partridge."

In 1970, the Catholic Church named Teresa a Doctor of the Church, meaning she was an eminent theologian. None of the other doctors are so earthy, so approachable, or so downright quirky.

For one thing, many theologians arrive at their conclusions after years of studying books. Not Teresa, who said she had learned much of what she knew through heavenly visions. Here's what she said about the person who is fortunate enough to receive such visions: "In a single instant he is taught so many things all at once that, if he were to labor for years on end in trying to fit them all into his imagination and thought, he could not succeed with a thousandth part of them."

Her books are unusual. She frequently loses her train of thought, takes the reader through long-winded digressions, mixes up her references to the Bible, and often complains about personal

people around them. She said the most reliable way to gain an understanding of people's spiritual maturity is by looking at their service to others. "We cannot be sure if we are loving God, although we may have good reasons for believing that we are, but we can know quite well if we are loving our neighbor."

Dorothy Day, the American activist and pacifist who cofounded the Catholic Worker movement, loved Teresa's pragmatism and

---

afflictions that make writing more difficult. "As I write this," she says at one point, "the noises in my head are so loud that I am beginning to wonder what is going on in it."

And what other Christian writer apologizes so frequently to her audience: "The reader must have patience with me as I have myself when writing about things of which I know nothing."

Still, Teresa's unique and lively writing style effectively communicates her passionate heart across the centuries while conveying complex thoughts in reader-friendly sound bites. Why does God even bother listening to our petitions? "The Lord's humility allows Him to be conquered by prayer," says Teresa. Why should we seek God with our hearts and not just our minds? "It is most harmful *not* to believe that God is powerful and can do works which are incomprehensible to our understanding," she writes.

In many ways, Teresa was a product of her time. Unfortunately, the sixteenth century was a time when the contributions of women were little valued and when wary church leaders were looking for heretics under every bed. But Teresa didn't let such obstacles stand in her way. As she writes in *Interior Castle:*

Oh, poor little butterfly, bound by so many fetters, which prevent you from flying whithersoever you will! Have pity on her, my God; and dispose things so that she may be able to do something towards fulfilling her desires to Thy honor and glory.

named her own daughter after the saint. "I had read the life of St. Teresa of Avila and fallen in love with her," writes Day in her autobiography, *The Long Loneliness*. "She was a mystic and a practical woman, a recluse and a traveler, a cloistered nun and yet most active."

Teresa often applied her practical insights to the most spiritual of matters. Following the advice of Jesus, she encouraged those who experienced periods of dryness and difficulty in their prayer life to keep at it. "If we are not quite sure that the King has heard us, or sees us, we must not stay where we are like ninnies," she says.

Mysticism can lead to excesses, and we have all heard about people who become so wrapped up in heavenly things that they are absolutely no earthly good. Teresa frequently chastised such heavenly minded souls, and by following her practical example we can learn how to find a healthy balance between the deep needs of our souls and the pressing demands that we face every day.

My 2000 album *Simple Heart* includes a song titled "God Alone Is Enough," which is based on a prayer of St. Teresa's. Perhaps as you meditate on these lyrics, you can seek God's will for the proper balance of the mystical and the practical in your own life.

> *Let nothing trouble you*
> *Let nothing frighten you*
> *Everything passes*
> *But God will never change*
> *God alone is enough*
> *God alone is enough*
> *Whoever has God*
> *Wants for nothing at all*
> *Patient endurance*
> *Will obtain everything*
> *Whoever has God*
> *Wants for nothing at all*
> *God alone is enough*

God alone is enough
Whoever has God
Wants for nothing at all

We can learn so many things from this wise and practical saint. She believed God wants to move and live within us. As a result, we don't have to contort ourselves by saying unusual prayers. We merely need to surrender to God's sovereign will. And of course, as a lifelong monastic, she believed community could help all of us along the road to spiritual growth.

God may never grant each one of us the opportunity to experience the things Teresa experienced. But that's OK. All we need to concentrate on is moving closer to him day by day. He can take care of everything from there.

LEARNING MORE ABOUT
Teresa of Avila

Some of the mystics featured in this book are either poor writers or their message is so complex that reading their original writing is too much of a challenge for average folks seeking spiritual guidance. But such is not the case with Teresa, whose *Interior Castle* is one of the most reader-friendly guides to the mystical life ever written.

Passages of deep earnestness are mixed with humorous statements that reveal Teresa's common humanness. There are many versions available, but we used the 1944 translation by E. Allison Peers—a scholar who focused much of his work on making the writings of the Spanish mystics (Ignatius, Teresa, and John) readily available to contemporary English-speaking audiences.

More recently, the HarperCollins Spiritual Classics series has released an inexpensive abridged version: *Teresa of Avila: Selections from the Interior Castle* (2004).

Cathleen Medwick was a features editor at *Vogue* and *Vanity Fair* magazines, and she brings her journalistic skills to bear in her accessible biography, *Teresa of Avila: The Progress of a Soul* (Doubleday, 1999, and Image, 2001).

"Saint Teresa of Avila: The Ironic Doctor" is a shorter biographical essay by Francine Prose. It is found in Paul Elie's *A Tremor of Bliss: Contemporary Writers on the Saints* (Harcourt, 1994). This chapter also mentioned Bert Ghezzi's book, *The Voices of the Saints: A Year of Readings* (Doubleday, 2000).

The Way of Darkness
John of the Cross

Today, the West is awash in the teachings of a popular and seemingly harmless "happy school" of Christianity that proclaims a feel-good gospel while neglecting the difficulties and challenges that often accompany the commitment to follow Christ.

This happy-school theology is heard in many of today's best-selling Christian recordings, which focus more on spiritual triumphalism and candy-colored contentedness than on the impact of sin or suffering in our lives and our world. It also fuels evangelism efforts that promise converts they will be better off materially or emotionally after they accept Christ, as well as efforts in megachurch marketing programs that aim to attract repeat "customers" by giving people precisely what they want, be it entertaining Sunday morning services or small groups focusing on their favorite hobbies and pastimes. The popular bumper-sticker slogan, "Smile, God loves you!" aptly summarizes the happy school's approach.

John of the Cross—a sixteenth-century Spanish monk who helped Teresa of Avila with her program of monastic reform and suffered mightily for his efforts—proclaims a more sober and world-weary approach to faith. An influential and in some ways tragic figure, John is perhaps Christendom's most acclaimed mystical theologian. His four-word summary of the gospel has little to do with the language of self-help spirituality and focuses instead on these haunting words of Jesus: "Take up your cross."

Don't get me wrong. God *does* love us. People *have* found comfort in faith for centuries. And joy *is* a Christian virtue. But does all this mean that happiness—however we define it—is the Christian's inalienable right? Christian martyrs, including both Catholics and the Protestants that fill John Foxe's *Book of Martyrs* didn't think so, nor did John of the Cross, whose mystical master-piece, *Dark Night of the Soul*, describes the sometimes agonizing inner ordeals we must endure as we are transformed into the kinds of people God desires as his most intimate companions.

Or as he said in one of his aphorisms: "The fly that clings to honey hinders its flight, and the soul that allows itself attach-ment to spiritual sweetness hinders its own liberty and contem-plation."

A Life in Limbo

The goal here, and in following sections, was to let the song lyrics themselves start the sections. We believe the attribution at the end of each set of lyrics will be sufficient. An explanation is provided at the end of the chapter.

Where Have You Hidden?

Where have you hidden, Beloved?
Why have You wounded my soul?
I went out to the wilderness calling for You
But You were gone
Oh shepherds keeping your watch in the hills
If by chance you meet with my Love
Tell Him I suffer in my lonely grief
And I soon will die
But I have searched for my Love in the mountains
I have searched among the meadows and the fields
He has poured out a thousand graces in them

So my heart might be healed
Yet my heart is not healed

—"Where Have You Hidden," from
The Lover and the Beloved, with lyrics
based on St. John of the Cross,
adapted by John Michael Talbot

Those who believe psychology shapes theology would have a field day investigating the biography of John of the Cross, which is punctuated by sadness and sorrow.

Born in 1542 at Fontiveros, a Spanish town located near Avila, John was less than a year old when his father died—a loss that forced the family into poverty and led to the death of an older brother, Luis, from starvation. His mother was unable to care for John, her youngest child, so she placed him in a boarding school for orphans run by Christian monks.

John died in 1591 after an attack of fever. For more than a year before his death, he endured a humiliating smear campaign instigated by fellow monks who opposed his leadership. They stripped him of his office, demoted him to the life of a simple monk, and circulated cruel rumors about him.

But in between his unstable youth and his troubled death, John enjoyed many years of study, teaching, and service to various monasteries. He also demonstrated a passionate commitment to God that only deepened as he aged. Ordained as a priest when he was about twenty-five years old, he was a devoted member of the Carmelite order, which was founded around 1200 on the western slope of the holy land's sacred Mount Carmel.

The earliest Carmelites were hermits and semi-hermits who banded together in communities, lived in obedience to their communal rule, and submitted to the leadership of a prior.

John had a strong desire to be a hermit, which may have influenced his decision to join the Carmelites. But a chance meeting

John and His Time

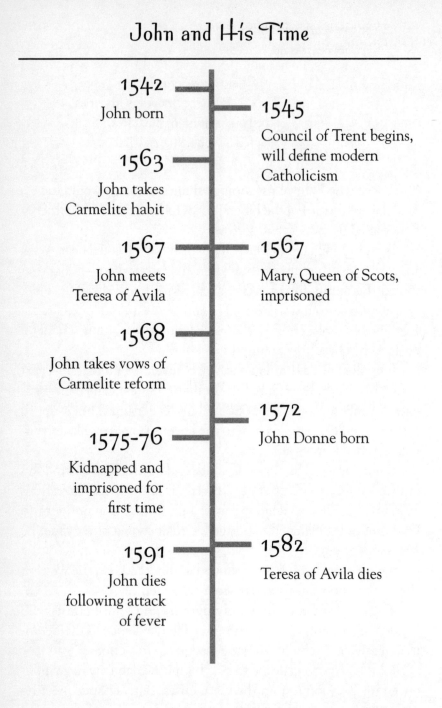

1542
John born

1545
Council of Trent begins,
will define modern
Catholicism

1563
John takes
Carmelite habit

1567
John meets
Teresa of Avila

1567
Mary, Queen of Scots,
imprisoned

1568
John takes vows of
Carmelite reform

1572
John Donne born

1575-76
Kidnapped and
imprisoned for
first time

1591
John dies
following attack
of fever

1582
Teresa of Avila dies

with a Carmelite sister named Teresa of Avila changed the course of his life, drawing him away from a life of solitary prayer and propelling him into a life of public service and controversy that would cause him no end of troubles for the rest of his life.

Teresa believed that Carmelites of her own day had strayed from the founders' commitment to solitude, simplicity, and contemplative prayer, and she began focusing more on teaching and service. She wanted to inspire members of the order to recover their founding commitments.

Beginning in 1562, she established a series of foundations that encouraged women to live quiet, prayer-filled lives. She met John in 1567 and immediately recognized in him a man who shared her spiritual commitments and could help promote her program of reform. John agreed to work with her and founded the first monastery for men in the new Discalced Carmelite order.

At the time, religious upheaval was in the air. In Catholic countries like Spain, a powerful counter-Reformation sought to counteract Europe's growing Protestant movement that advocated a complete break from the Catholic Church. And although many Catholics supported reform, some of the leaders in the Carmelite order did not.

One of John's most persistent prayers was that God would enable him "to suffer and be despised," and his opponents in the Carmelite order helped answer that prayer in spades. These opponents targeted John for a series of reprisals and attacks. They repeatedly kidnapped him, confining him in dreary prisons and subjecting him to horrible torture.

His final and harshest imprisonment came when he was hidden deep within the bowels of a Carmelite monastery in Toledo for half a year. His cramped cell was so cold that he developed frostbite. His diet was so skimpy that anyone less accustomed to fasting might have given up in despair. And to make matters worse, his captors regularly beat him.

Completely closed off from the outside world, John was disheartened when his captors falsely claimed that the reforms he and Teresa were promoting had been overturned by a new pope.

Unable to do anything else in his captivity, John prayed and began composing poems in his head. When he was moved to a less confining cell, a sympathetic guard gave him paper and a pen, and John began writing his poems down.

Prisons have served as workshops for some of the world's great literature, including Thoreau's powerful essay "Civil Disobedience," some of Gandhi's works on passive resistance, and Martin Luther King Jr.'s "Letter from a Birmingham Jail." John's long periods of enforced silence and meditation helped inspire the composition of two of the Western world's most treasured spiritual classics. *Dark Night of the Soul* and its companion volume, *Ascent of Mount Carmel* (henceforth referred to as *Dark Night* and *Ascent*) began as a series of prison poems that portray the spiritual seeker as a bride whose longing for her lover—the Divine Bridegroom—drives her on until her desired union is perfectly consummated.

After he finally escaped from his cell at Toledo, John wrote lengthy commentaries on his poems. These commentaries, which were originally intended for interested monks and nuns in the Discalced Carmelite order, spell out his detailed views on the mystical life. Thus through his poetry and his prose commentaries, John gives us a depth of understanding and insight into the spiritual journey that has rarely—if ever—been matched by other writers.

He was not the first writer to explore the riches of so-called spousal mysticism. The Apostle Paul frequently employed bride-bridegroom imagery, as did St. Augustine, who was probably Christianity's most influential theologian. We have also seen in earlier chapters that both St. Bernard and St. Francis frequently compared the spiritual life to a relationship of covenantal love. But John dives into these matters more deeply than others do.

One of the occupational challenges mystics face is describing in puny words the all-encompassing experiences they enjoy. The bride-bridegroom analogy helps explain these often-complex topics. That's why I called my own first book on spiritual matters *The Lover and the Beloved*. I also composed music for a companion recording, and I am using the lyrics from this album, which are based on John's poems, throughout this chapter.

I have found that some of the words Christian mystics have written over the ages can be twisted beyond recognition by fearful fundamentalists or used as a form of self-defense by well-meaning but misguided mystics. But bride-bridegroom imagery, particularly as it is spelled out by John of the Cross, can help guide our spiritual lives into practices that are both healthy and appropriate.

Via Negativa

One Dark Night

One dark night
Fueled with love's urgent longings
I went out unseen
My house being all, now still
On that glad night
In the secret, for no one saw me
Nor did I see any other thing at all
With no other light to guide me
Than the Light burning in my heart

> —"One Dark Night," from *The Lover and the Beloved*

There's another type of imagery that has become synonymous with John's approach to the spiritual life, and I believe an anecdote from his life can help us understand this approach.

John was a close friend, spiritual brother, and devoted associate of Teresa of Avila, and the two worked together on monastic reform for fifteen years and often shared ideas about the mystical life until her death in 1582. During that time, they exchanged many letters, some of which meant so much to John that he carried them with him for many years. Then one day John burned his prized letters from Teresa. Why? He felt he had become so attached to them that they were interfering with his spiritual growth.

John believed that attachments are a major reason people fail to progress in the Christian life. They want to move closer to God, but other things claim their affections and limit their zeal for God. John explained in *Ascent* that only by undergoing a "dark night" journey that removes all competing attachments can we attain the union with God we seek:

> We may say that there are three reasons for which this journey made by the soul to union with God is called night. The first has to do with the point from which the soul goes forth, for it has gradually to deprive itself of desire for all the worldly things which it possessed, by denying them to itself; the which denial and deprivation are, as it were, night to all the senses of man. The second reason has to do with the mean, or the road along which the soul must travel to this union—that is, faith, which is likewise as dark as night to the understanding. The third has to do with the point to which it travels—namely, God, Who, equally, is dark night to the soul in this life. These three nights must pass through the soul—or, rather, the soul must pass through them—in order that it may come to Divine union with God.

Theologians have a name for John's approach. They call it *apophatic* or negative theology. Apophatic teachers like John say that before we approach God, we must first own up to the fact that all our ideas and concepts about God may be completely erroneous and may actually hinder us from reaching him as he is.

There are hints of the apophatic approach near the conclusion of Paul's famous love passage in his first letter to the Corinthians. "Now we see but a poor reflection as in a mirror," writes Paul. "Then we shall see face to face. Now I know in part; then I shall know fully, even as I am fully known" (1 Corinthians 13:12). Later, theologians such as Dionysius the Pseudo-Areopagite and Gregory of Nyssa further developed these ideas. And in books like the anonymous English work, *The Cloud of Unknowing*, the apophatic is taken to extremes that some theologians consider dangerous.

John didn't take things that far, but he did insist that only by going through a "dark night" process that could take "some years" would we be stripped of our false assumptions and natural predispositions, enabling us to encounter God in spirit and in truth. "No thing, created or imagined, can serve the understanding as a proper means of union with God," he writes, particularly if we "cling to it." John tells us to put away all intellectual constructs and vain imaginings in order to "learn to abide attentively and wait lovingly upon God in that state of quiet."

Throughout *Ascent*, John describes a number of specific attachments that impede the growth of our relationship with God. The Bible calls pride the "original sin," and according to John its descendents are "self-esteem and vain presumption." Those who fall victim to such spiritual pride routinely think themselves better than other Christians, "taking more delight in their own spirituality and spiritual gifts than those of others."

John spends many chapters of *Ascent* discussing the dangers inherent in many of the blessings people enjoy. John believes there are six types of blessings—temporal, natural, sensual, moral, supernatural, and spiritual—and each category carries its own unique risks.

Temporal blessings include riches, which some of us believe are a means to serve God. But John says they are an offence to God. Likewise, he claims the desire to have children is "vain" and can detract from loving God.

Natural blessings like "beauty, grace, comeliness, bodily constitution and all other bodily endowments" can lead to "vainglory, presumption, pride and disesteem of our neighbor" if we allow ourselves to believe these things are our own instead of the unmerited gifts of God. Such presumption and pride have led to "the fall of many holy men."

Even spiritual things can be a source of confusion and error. Good works are not so good if done for the applause of men. Portraits of saints, fancy chapels, and pompous ceremonies can be the cause of vanity rather than true worship. Rosaries and other aids to prayer can delude us if we become caught up in their craft instead of what they represent. Pilgrimages to holy places can be harmful if they are undertaken "for recreation rather than devotion." And depending on each person's motives, religious festivals can either help us worship God or can cause our downfall if we use them primarily to make business contacts or to glory in "seeing or being seen."

John concludes that the safest rituals and practices are those that a person can practice where it is "solitary and wild"—places that have the least to do with this world. "The person who is truly devout sets his devotion principally upon that which is invisible," he writes.

The Soul's Ascent

I Found My Beloved

So I found my Beloved in the mountains
On the lonely and far distant isles
O'er resounding waters
I heard the whispering
Of love's breezes to heal my broken heart
Oh tranquil evening
Silent music
And the sounding solitude of the rising dawn
It is there that I hear You
There that I taste of You
In love's banquet to fill my heart

—"I Found My Beloved," from *The Lover and the Beloved*

If we stopped our discussion of John's mysticism here, focusing only on his ideas about the soul's passage through this dark night of purgation, you would only get a partial and inaccurate image of his theology. But John wrote about more than darkness and self-denial. In fact, the main goal of his writing was to usher his readers into the light.

John explains his goal nearly two-thirds of the way through *Ascent,* and although it might have been nice to read this information earlier in the book, getting it late is better than not getting it at all:

> The discreet reader has ever need to bear in mind the intent and end which I have in this book, which is the direction of the soul, through all its apprehensions, natural and supernatural without deception or hindrance, in purity of faith, to Divine union with God.

John expands on his approach elsewhere in *Ascent* and *Dark Night:* "Ascending to the summit of the Mount . . . is the high estate of perfection which we here call union of the soul with God." All the painful processes of purgation are designed to serve this higher end. "Although these purgations seem to blind the spirit, they do so only to enlighten it again with a brighter and intenser light, which it is preparing itself to receive with greater abundance." Or as he writes elsewhere, "Being empty, (the soul) is able indeed to be poor in spirit and freed from the old man, in order to live that new and blessed life which is attained by means of this night, and which is the state of union with God."

But if his goal is positive, why does John spend so much time and energy on the negative? It's because he believes only those souls willing to venture through a dark night of preparation will truly make progress on the path to perfection.

"God dwells substantially in every soul, even in that of the greatest sinner in the world," he writes. But "God communicates Himself most to that soul that has progressed farthest in love; namely, that has its will in closest conformity with the will of God."

We hope that our time in the dark night will prepare us for the light of a brighter day. "The first and principal benefit caused by this arid and dark night of contemplation (is) the knowledge of oneself and one's misery," he writes. Such knowledge, if properly understood and applied, can help us move from the state of "beginners" to the state of "progressives" who have their feet on the path and are making steady progress up the Mount of Perfection.

John may spend more time on the theme of darkness than other mystics, but there is solid biblical precedent for his emphasis on self-denial. In the gospel of Mark, Jesus explains that following him comes at great cost. "If anyone would come after me, he must deny himself and take up his cross and follow me. For whoever wants to save his life will lose it, but whoever loses his life for me and for the gospel will save it" (Mark 8:34–35). Jesus makes similar claims in Luke's gospel: "Any of you who does not give up everything he has cannot be my disciple," he tells his disciples (Luke 14:33).

Many of us may prefer uplifting sermons, inspirational books, or upbeat gospel music that promotes a more happy-Christianity take on Jesus' radical, revolutionary message, but John understood the often-neglected side of the gospel message.

A Powerful, Perplexing Message

I Know a Well

I know a well that flows and runs
Yet remains hidden
Eternal spring, a hidden well
Yet I know where it rises
I do not know where it begins
For it is eternal
Every beginning and every end
Flow from this well

—"I Know a Well," from The Lover
and the Beloved

John was a controversial figure in his day. Not only did some of his Carmelite brothers imprison and torture him, but some of his books were investigated by the Spanish Inquisition, which ultimately judged his work to be free of doctrinal error. Within a century and a half after his death, John was named a saint. Two centuries later, he was named a Doctor of the Church.

Still, it's important for us to assess the complex legacy of this towering saint. Let's begin with his unique and often difficult writing style. John was the kind of writer who never used one word when two would do. He preferred long sentences over short ones and convoluted paragraphs over elegant ones. And he was never content with explaining a concept once when he could attack it in a dozen different ways in a dozen different locations.

Though John's writing is far more systematic than Teresa's, it is also more dense, more confusing, and more infuriating to read. John's books are cloaked in lofty, learned rhetoric that sometimes seems at odds with the passionate spiritual realities he is straining to describe.

However, his writing does share one important trait with Teresa's essays on the spiritual life. Both writers fiercely attacked themselves in their own work, serving as their own harshest critics. "If any persons find themselves disagreeing with this instruction," John writes at one point, "it will be due to my ignorance and poor style." Elsewhere, John condemns himself for his "rude style and lack of knowledge," and admits, "I often write at too great length and go beyond the limits which are necessary for that part of the doctrine which I am treating."

Is John being overly hard on himself? Perhaps, for there are certainly moments when his writing can be both powerful and compelling. But sometimes when reading his work, such moments seem few and far between.

As for the content of his writing, there's no question that John's negative, apophatic theology and his detailed description of the way of darkness make an essential contribution to the literature of Christian mysticism. I believe his thoughts on the dark night of the

Testing the Spirits

In his first epistle, St. John cautioned his readers to be wise about spiritual things. "Dear friends, do not believe every spirit," he wrote, "but test the spirits to see whether they are from God, because many false prophets have gone out into the world" (1 John 4:1).

Christians of all kinds have been trying to follow John's advice ever since, but the challenge of testing the spirits is even more crucial for mystics who, by their nature, have experiences that others do not share. Mystics undergo locutions, visions, revelations, and other experiences. But how do they distinguish insights that truly come from God and those that are less trustworthy?

For John of the Cross, there was one simple answer, and it involved testing supernatural revelations against the revelation already given to us by God in the Scriptures. "I shall trust neither to experience nor to knowledge, since both may fail and deceive," he wrote. "But, while not omitting to make such use as I can of these two things, I shall avail myself . . . of Divine Scripture; for if we guide ourselves by this, we shall be unable to stray, since He Who speaks therein is the Holy Spirit."

As John saw it, there's no need to look to heaven for answers to many of our deepest questions because God has already answered them in his Son.

> It is not fitting, then, to enquire of God by supernatural means, nor is it necessary that He should answer; since all the faith has been given us in Christ, and there is therefore no more of it to be revealed, nor will there be.

Both John and Teresa of Avila wrote frequently about the dangers of spiritual delusion and the power of supernatural experiences—in all their varied forms—to lead innocent souls astray. As he put it:

Although all these things may happen . . . we must never rely upon them or accept them, but must always fly from them. . . . He that esteems such things errs greatly and exposes himself to great peril of being deceived.

John's mystical writings contain dozens of stern warnings. Those who lust for "sweetness and delectable communion with God" are guilty of "spiritual gluttony." Those who dabble in prophecies about future events are dancing with the devil, who knows a thing or two about what will happen tomorrow and is only too willing to entice us with such knowledge.

People who harbor spiritual pride are particularly vulnerable, since they may confuse their own ideas or notions with God's truth.

Although sayings and revelations may be of God, we cannot always be sure of their meaning, in part because of the defective ways in which we understand them. . . . To desire to commune with God by such means is a most perilous thing.

Such arguments may sound theoretical, but they're not. John was "appalled" by some of the cases of spiritual delusion he had seen among the monks and nuns he supervised. "I knew a person who had these successive locutions: among them were some very true and substantial ones concerning the most holy Sacrament of the Eucharist, but others were sheer heresy."

So what's a true seeker after God to do? John's advice here is consistent with the rest of his counsel. "It must neither desire to have them, nor desire not to have them; but must merely be humble and resigned concerning them, and God will perform His work how and when He wills."

soul are especially relevant today—a time when a tsunami of happy Christianity threatens to drown out more serious and demanding approaches to the Christian life.

But those who are not serious students of mystical literature should handle certain aspects of John's teaching with care. One is his seeming insistence that physical existence, with all its attendant needs and desires, is inherently sinful. John states that "the person who is truly devout sets his devotion principally upon that which is invisible." But St. Francis, who readily saw the fingerprints of the Creator throughout creation, would differ with John on this point, as would other mystics in this book. Bodily desires and lusts have distracted many people and seduced some from pursuing their highest spiritual callings, but that does not mean physicality itself is sinful.

In addition, John's emphasis on the process of the dark night seems to have similarities to a doctrine known as Quietism, which contains teachings that have been judged heretical. In its most radical form, Quietism (a doctrine that has sometimes been referred to as Illuminism) teaches that spiritual growth is a matter of God's doing, not ours, and that all human effort toward spiritual growth is misguided or counterproductive.

John is not a Quietist. In fact, he argues that our spiritual growth is a result of a partnership between human and divine agencies.

> The truth, I repeat, is that God must place the soul in this supernatural state; but the soul, as far as in it lies, must be continually preparing itself; and this it can do by natural means, especially with the help that God is continually giving it.

Following in John's Footsteps

As we have seen in this brief summary of John's towering work, love and darkness represent the two poles of his theology. Love, as described in his imagery of the Lover and the Beloved, represents the positive side of the spiritual pilgrimage we must all take toward

God. God is love, and he created us with the capability to love him. But as too often happens, things that are less worthy of our devotion impinge on our love for God.

In our human relationships with friends, members of our Christian community, a spouse, or our children, love is something that requires time, attention, and selfless dedication. We cannot assume that love will grow and develop on its own, but we must instead nurture it and cultivate it with every fiber of our being.

The same is true in our love relationship with God. Every day we must seek to love God more deeply, more purely, and more fully. One way to do this is to ask God to increase our longing for him day by day until that longing for him replaces the desires and hungers we have for so many other things.

We must also be willing to endure the dark nights of the soul that John describes so powerfully. None of us likes it when our cherished ideals or our notions of our own personal identity come crashing down around us. But if we are patient in trouble and persevere in our love of God, we will be privileged to see new birth taking place in our souls, bit by bit. And over time, God will use the trials and tribulations of our life to remake us in the image of his Son.

LEARNING MORE ABOUT
John of the Cross

As with Teresa, we have relied on E. Allison Peers's faithful and readable translations of John's two major works, *Dark Night of the Soul* (Doubleday/Image, 1959/1990) and *Ascent of Mount Carmel* (Image, 1958). Other worthwhile translations are also available, but the authoritative version remains *The Collected Works of St. John of the Cross*, translated by Kieran Kavanaugh, OCD, and Otilio Rodriguez, OCD, (ICS Publications, 1991). Contemporary readers may prefer the recently released *John of the Cross: Selections from* The Dark Night *and Other Writings* (2004), a volume in the HarperCollins Spiritual Classics series.

Allison Peers is the author of two additional titles: *Handbook to the Life and Times of St. Teresa and St. John* (1953) and *Studies of the Spanish Mystics* (1927). A more recent study is R. A. Herrera's *Silent Music: The Life, Work, and Thought of St. John of the Cross* (Eerdmans, 2003).

It has been interesting to see how John's work is being embraced by contemporary Christian counselors. Gerald G. May, author of the popular book *Addiction and Grace*, has written *The Dark Night of the Soul: A Psychiatrist Explores the Connection Between Darkness and Spiritual Growth* (HarperSanFrancisco, 2003). And evangelical counselor Larry Crabb wrote an essay on John in Scott Larsen's *Indelible Ink: 22 Prominent Christian Leaders Discuss the Books That Shape Their Faith* (WaterBrook, 2003).

I also explore John's approach in *The Lover and the Beloved* (Crossroads, 1985) and the companion musical recording. I have quoted songs from this album throughout this chapter.

The Way of the Artist

John Donne and England's Metaphysical Poets

Was John Donne the greatest poet to ever write in the English language? Literary scholars continue to debate that question, as they do many other issues surrounding this complex, confusing, controversial, and seemingly contradictory artist. A poet, a prose stylist, and later the most influential preacher of his day, Donne created a vast body of work, some of which is well known, even among people who have never heard his name.

Millions of school children and upper-level literature students have read these timeless lines from his Holy Sonnet No. 10:

> *Death be not proud, though some have called thee*
> *Mighty and dreadful, for thou art not so. . . .*

In the poem's final line, Donne elegantly expresses the profound hope that has inspired Christians for twenty centuries: "And death shall be no more; death, thou shalt die."

Anyone familiar with Ernest Hemingway's novel *For Whom the Bell Tolls* has heard at least a tiny portion of "Devotions Upon Emergent Occasions," one of Donne's most famous prose works. Once again he was meditating upon death, but this time it was his own. Confined to his bed by a grave illness, Donne heard the sound of church bells sounding for another man's funeral. He wondered about the impact of one soul's departure on those of us who remain, and as he wondered, he wrote:

No man is an island, entire of itself; every man is a piece of the continent, a part of the main. If a clod be washed away by the sea, Europe is the less, as well as if a promontory were, as well as if a manor of thy friend's or thine own were. Any man's death diminishes me because I am involved in mankind, and therefore never send to know for whom the bell tolls, it tolls for thee.

Some might be tempted to call Donne morbid, but he wasn't. Rather, as one critic put it, he had a lifelong fascination with "the paradoxical human union of spirit and matter."

The famous line, "Go and catch a falling star" was Donne's, too. It's the opening salvo of "Song," one of his cynical love poems that compares a series of impossible feats to the most difficult task of all: finding a woman who is "true and fair."

The Mystery of Art

Years ago, I wrote a book titled *The Master Musician*. In this book, I tried to point out some of the more intriguing connections between art and mysticism. As noted earlier, a mystic is a person who experiences an extraordinary connection to God. And some people believe artists are mystics of a kind. That can be debated, but in the case of Donne the argument is more clear-cut. He was an artist who, over the course of a long and troubled life, sought to use his art for the glory of God. Thinking about Donne's life and his work, I was reminded of one of the early passages in *The Master Musician*:

God is the Master Musician. We are his instruments. He gently plucks the strings of our lives to make a harmonious song for all creation. We are like a beautifully crafted guitar, formed, sanded, seasoned, lacquered, and brought to expression by the same hand.

God does not require perfection in his instruments. The only thing required is that we willingly submit to the hand of our Master.

Donne was born in 1572 (eight years after Shakespeare) and died in 1641 (twenty-five years after Shakespeare). Both writers were born into devoted Catholic families who struggled to find a safe haven for their faith at a time when England's Protestant Reformation was solidifying its gains. The nation's religious and political leaders were subjecting Catholics to persecution, taking their homes and property, or executing them. And Donne, who would later join the Anglican church, may have felt the brunt of this harassment more than Shakespeare did, as Donne was a distant relative of St. Thomas More, the holy man who had stood up to King Henry VIII and paid with his life.

Some literary critics suggest that Donne did for poetry what Shakespeare did for drama: he stretched its technical limitations, broadened the themes it explored, and raised the bar for all future writers. But what makes him a valid subject for this book is the way that he, perhaps more than any other major Western writer, gave himself over, in both his life and his work, to exploring the varied ways God and humans interact.

He is widely regarded as the first and greatest representative of a literary movement known as the metaphysical school. As poets know all too well, words are slippery things. Today, the term *metaphysical* is primarily associated with New Age spirituality or esoteric philosophy.

Donne never applied the term to himself. Rather, it's a label that John Dryden and Samuel Johnson applied to Donne and to later English poets like Robert Herrick, George Herbert, Andrew Marvell, and Thomas Traherne (see the sidebar). These poets shared a love of verbal wit and intellectual gamesmanship, a weakness for elaborate metaphors, and a belief that poetry could be a vehicle for exploring some of humanity's most complex philosophical questions about life, love, and death. Often their poetry could be difficult to understand, but for them, difficult was good.

Today, Donne is remembered as one of the world's greatest poets and preachers, but such a description would have shocked

John Donne and His Time

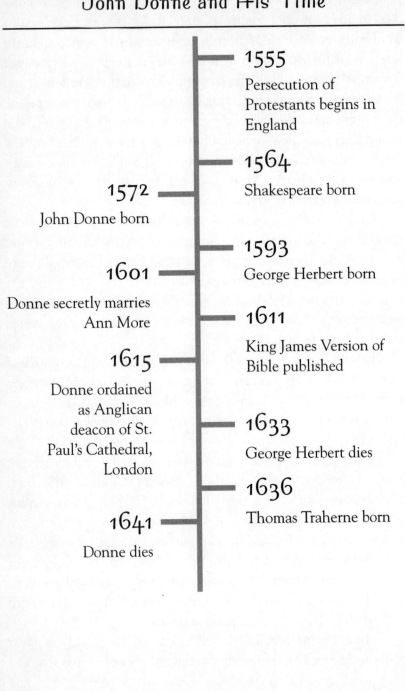

1555
Persecution of
Protestants begins in
England

1564
Shakespeare born

1572
John Donne born

1593
George Herbert born

1601
Donne secretly marries
Ann More

1611
King James Version of
Bible published

1615
Donne ordained
as Anglican
deacon of St.
Paul's Cathedral,
London

1633
George Herbert dies

1636
Thomas Traherne born

1641
Donne dies

those who knew the youthful John Donne as a playboy, a rogue, and possibly a pornographer.

How did a sex-obsessed young man become one of the towering figures of English literature and Anglican spirituality? Donne sometimes wondered the same thing himself. "Oh, to vex me," he wrote in one of his Holy Sonnets, "contraries meet in one."

Unraveling the mystery of the various John Donnes will require us to examine three separate but related characters who inhabited three distinct periods of his life. First, there's the young and sexually adventurous "Jack" Donne. Next, there's the happily married but poverty-stricken John Donne of middle age. And finally, there's the older and wiser Dr. Donne—a preacher to kings and an intimate friend of God.

Young Jack Donne: An Oversexed Playboy?

Most of the mystics featured in this book used erotic imagery as a metaphor to describe the soul's union with God. For the young Jack Donne, sexual imagery wasn't metaphorical; it was graphic, and it was real—so real one can hear the rustling of sheets and the panting of breathless lovers in the background: "Off with that girdle," he commands his partner in "Elegy XIX, Going to Bed."

> Full nakedness! All joys are due to thee,
> As souls unbodied, bodies unclothed must be.

In "The Canonization," Donne employs the language of sanctity to describe sex and urges his partner to worship in silence: "For God's sake hold your tongue, and let me love."

His poem, "The Ecstasy," did not describe the spiritual raptures St. Teresa of Avila wrote about:

> Love these mixed souls doth mix again,
> And makes both one, each this and that.

Over the course of dozens and dozens of poems, virgins are deflowered, prostitutes are bedded, eligible young women are seduced and then abandoned. One poem, "Elegy 19: To His Mistress Going to Bed," employs imagery of explorers like Christopher Columbus to describe a sexual romp that may have involved the wife of a close associate:

> License my roving hands, and let them go
> Before, behind, between, above, below.
> O my America, my newfound land,
> My kingdom safeliest when with one man manned.

Such sentiments led the Christian writer and literary scholar C. S. Lewis to call at least one of Donne's poems pornographic. Lewis, who explained his position in his essay, "Donne and Love Poetry in the Seventeenth Century," sounded a bit like modern-day critics who object to the salacious nature of pop music lyrics performed by recording artists like Prince and Madonna or, more recently, rap and hip-hop artists. "I mean by it," wrote Lewis in one case, "that this poem, in my opinion, is intended to arouse the appetite it describes, to affect not only the imagination but the nervous system of the reader."

But in many of Donne's poems, it is clear that the sex is more than merely physical. In "The Good-Morrow," two lovers awake after a passionate night together, and the poet wonders what life was like before they met.

> I wonder, by my troth, what thou and I
> Did, till we loved?

And in the next verse, Donne sings the redemptive power of love:

> For love all love of other sights controls,
> And makes one little room an everywhere.

Scholar David Edwards says that although Donne's poems may have been explicit, the author was actually more interested in people's souls than their bodies.

"He is . . . a poet of love," writes Edwards in *John Donne: Man of Flesh and Spirit*, "never describing physical beauty in detail but brilliantly able to recreate a man's experience of love's emotions and realities." Or as Donne himself said, his poems were the product of a "feeling brain."

Donne's erotic poems, many of which were written for the amusement of male friends at Cambridge and Oxford, were not published until after his death. Almost immediately, people began debating whether such explicit writing sprang from personal experience or merely an overheated imagination. This debate continues today in literary circles, at Donne conferences, and in the pages of the scholarly *John Donne Journal*.

Donne later dismissed his early poems as "rags," and he did little to preserve them (whereas he lavished great care over the preservation of the many sermons he delivered in the final phase of his life). Perhaps writing erotic verse was one way for Donne to keep his mind off the religious controversies that were unsettling Europe and had led to the death of his brother Henry, who died of the plague in Newgate prison, where he had been sentenced for harboring a Catholic priest.

But if his goal was to escape his inner turmoil, there were times when he realized that sex was an insufficient drug for deadening his pain. In some of his poems, Donne described the feeling of pervasive emptiness that followed some of his romantic exploits. Writing in "Farewell to Love," he regrets that the joy of sex is often followed by "A kind of sorrowing dullness to the mind."

Donne never ceased to be fascinated by sex, but his interest in love poetry eventually gave way to concerns about finding a career, and he finally landed a plum job as the private secretary to Sir Thomas Egerton, the Lord Keeper of England. Donne enjoyed the security of his new life but was troubled by the moral compromises politics entailed. "We cry out upon the illness of the times and we make the times ill," he wrote.

If he had played his cards right, Donne may have settled into a comfortable career as a government bureaucrat. But this passionate young man was about to make a radical move that would change his life forever.

Mr. John Donne: The (Mostly) Happily Married Man

In December of 1601, Donne made one of the rashest moves of his life. He secretly married Ann More, who was the daughter of his employer's brother-in-law. At the time, Donne was twenty-nine; Ann was seventeen. Two months later, Donne confessed his marriage to Sir Egerton and was immediately dismissed from his position and imprisoned. Only a judge's verdict that the marriage was legitimate saved Donne's skin.

The next fifteen years were some of the happiest and most difficult in Donne's life. He and Ann shared a love that was deep and passionate. He even wrote poems about their marital bliss, some of which rival his earlier poetry for its literary elegance and erotic energy.

But life was hard, and the little money they had was stretched thin trying to take care of nine children. Donne did some writing, but none of it paid very well. And he had no luck in securing steady work.

Donne had always been moody, but now a dark depression set in that not even the beauties of nature in springtime could dispel. "Everything refreshes and I wither," he wrote. Things got so bad that he wrote an essay titled *Biathantos* that offered a defense of suicide. In the unpublished work, Donne concluded that even though suicide was a sin, God could forgive it in the most desperate situations.

Some of Donne's well-placed friends urged him to do what other well educated but underemployed men had done: take holy orders and become a priest in the Church of England. But Donne refused. He declared that he was morally unworthy of such a position, and his own sense of worthlessness and inner spiritual turmoil may have influenced this decision.

That spiritual turmoil was reflected in the poem titled "Good Friday, 1613. Riding Westward." Here Donne described the beauties of Christ, who turns the wheels of the cosmos with his nail-pierced hands; Donne often uses the same finely wrought language he had previously used to describe his sexual escapades. The central theme of the poem is the idea of turning, or conversion. And Donne, who out of shame has had his back turned toward Christ, offers to present himself fully to his Master:

> *Burn off my rusts, and my deformity,*
> *Restore thine image, so much, by thy grace,*
> *That thou mayest know me, and I'll turn my face.*

A year later, Donne would become a member of the Church of England and be named a chaplain to King James I. This was the same James who would commission the Authorized (King James) version of the Bible. In 1615, he was ordained as an Anglican priest and deacon of St. Paul's Cathedral in London, the most important church in England.

Deciding to enter the ministry ended Donne's financial woes, but it would not bring him the happy, settled life he longed for. In August of 1617, Ann delivered the second of two stillborn children. She died five days later. This, combined with the recent death of Donne's daughter Mary and son Francis, caused him to place his soul in God's hands in ways he had never done before.

Dr. John Donne: Naked Before God

In the winter of 1623, Donne took ill. Doctors were called in, but the prognosis was not good, so he did what he had always done whenever he wanted to understand his own unruly thoughts and feelings: he grabbed paper and pen and began writing.

Donne survived this close brush with death. And his "Devotions Upon Emergent Occasions"—the collection of meditations he wrote from what he thought was his deathbed—yielded not only the phrase "for whom the bell tolls" but also a new level of intimacy in his relationship with God.

Full of prayers uttered from the depths of infirmity, the "Devotions" reveal a man laid low by physical ailments but still raising his soul to God: "Though thou have weakened my bodily knees, that they cannot bow to thee, hast yet left me the knees of my heart, which are bowed unto thee evermore; as thou hast made this bed thine altar."

After he regained his health and returned to the pulpit of St. Paul's, Donne's preaching was empowered by a deeper sense of passion and urgency. In one of his sermons, Donne alluded to disputes between Anglicans and Catholics about whether to endorse forms of self-denial that had been a part of the Catholic spiritual experience for centuries. "I am a Papist," he said, with a preacher's calculated effort to shock his listeners into hearing what he said. "That is, I will fast and pray as much as any Papist and enable my selfe for the service of my God, as seriously, as sedulously, as laboriously as any Papist."

In another sermon, he gave even more detail about the mystical devotion to Christ that was at the heart of his spiritual experience:

> I locke my doore to my selfe, and I throw my self downe in the presence of my God. I devest my selfe of all worldly thoughts, and I bend all my powers and faculties upon God, as I think, and suddenly I find my selfe scattered, melted, fallen into vaine thoughts, into no thoughts; I am upon my knees, and I talke, and think nothing.

The members of his congregation included lords and ladies, judges and lawyers, and virtually everybody who was anybody in the royal retinue. But as he told them in one of his hundreds of sermons, they would all be dead someday, just like the kings and queens of the past whose bones filled the stately crypts that lined St. Paul's massive marble corridors.

Death and illness were not abstractions for Donne's parishioners. Many had buried loved ones killed by the plague. In his sermons, Donne tried to bring home the reality of death in a way that would make his hearers reconsider how they lived and what they lived for. "The ashes of an Oak in the Chimney are no Epitaph of that Oak, to tell me how high or large that was," he told them. "It tells me not what flocks it sheltered while it stood or what men it hurt when it fell. The dust of great persons in the grave is speechless, it says nothing, it distinguishes nothing."

Some may have thought Donne was being too frank; others criticized the lofty language he used in many of his sermons. He responded by saying he had been called to serve his Master, just like Jesus' first disciples had. And like them, he would use any gifts and skills he had acquired in Christ's service. "They did leave their nets, but they did not burn them," he said.

He preached often about sin but always tried to do so in ways that acknowledged his own failings and offered hope and encouragement to fellow sinners. "True Instruction," said the former poet of passion, "is making love to the Congregation, and to every soul in it."

Donne returned again to the theme of death in the sermon he prepared for the First Friday in Lent, 1631. That sermon, titled "Death's Duel," may be the most famous of the hundreds he preached. It was also his last.

As he saw his own end coming nearer, a friend asked Donne why he was sad. The answer says a lot about the man:

> I am not sad, but most of the night past I have entertained myself with many thoughts of several friends that have left me here, and are gone to that place from which they shall not return; and that within a few days I also shall go hence, and be no more seen. . . . I was in serious contemplation of the providence and goodness of God to me. . . . And though of myself I have nothing to present to him but sins and misery, yet I know he looks not upon me now as I am of myself, but as I am in my Savior, and hath given me, even at

The Other Metaphysical Poets

Augustine Baker was a seventeenth-century English mystic who praised the power of poetry: "Various, yea infinite . . . are the ways of God, and various are the devices in the religious poet's armory of praise and self-analysis, and various his techniques for communicating his experience to his readers."

His description could have fit John Donne but would also describe the work of George Herbert, who was a friend of Donne's, and Thomas Traherne, who was born six years after Donne died. Like Donne, both men were Anglican clergymen. In addition, both were all too happy to discard the strict rules of the Elizabethan sonnet form and explore the challenge of writing poetry in bold, new, and exciting ways.

Herbert had wanted to carve out a career for himself in England's royal court before turning his back on the allurements of this life to become a part-time humble country parson and full-time philosopher and poet. His nonfiction book, *A Priest to the Temple; or, The Country Parson*, presents a somewhat idealized guide to parish life from a man who encouraged other pastors to serve their parishioners with all their hearts: "He shoots higher that threatens the moon, than he that aims at a tree," he wrote.

Herbert was a devout and holy man and a dedicated pastor, but most people remember him for his moving poetry, most of which was published shortly after his death in a collection titled *The Temple*. "The Elixir" serves as an example of his work:

> *Teach me, my God and King,*
> *In all things thee to see,*

THE WAY OF THE ARTIST   163

And what I do in anything
To do it as for thee.

Traherne was a Puritan preacher who became an Anglican priest. And though he lived and wrote in the seventeenth century, his work was unknown until it was accidentally discovered in the twentieth. After his poems and a prose collection, *Centuries of Meditations*, were published, excited readers declared him one of the greatest poets of his era.

Traherne saw God in every blade of grass and every beam of sunlight, and his work conveys a powerful sense of awe, wonder, and joy. Or as he expressed it in one of his poems:

How easily doth nature teach the soul!
How irresistible is her infusion
My senses were informers to my heart,
the conduits of his glory, power, and art.
. . . in God's works are hid the excellence
of such transcendent treasures.

It is fascinating to me how devout men like Donne, Herbert, Traherne, and others remade the poetry of their day. May a new generation of artists be inspired by their examples to do the same in all the varied arts today.

this present time, some testimonies by his Holy Spirit, that I am of the number of his elect: I am therefore full of inexpressible joy and shall die in peace.

The Song of Creation

In his poems and his sermons, Donne liked to speculate that the "word" by which God created the cosmos was a song. As a musician, I can sing a hearty "amen" to that sentiment. But you don't have to be a musician or poet or artist to sing along with me. God is the Master Musician who sang the universe into being and who would like to craft your soul into a beautiful instrument that makes music for his glory.

I have played many guitars in my life, from poorly made five-and-dime models to custom-crafted masterpieces. But I have found that the tone of the music is not based on the quality of a musical instrument but in the qualities of the musician who is playing it. A real artist can make beautiful music on even the cheapest instrument, while a bad musician will sound sour, even when playing on a beautifully crafted guitar. Likewise, God can create beautiful music out of our lives, no matter how flawed or failure-prone we think we are.

But there is a deeper mystery here. Each one of us is created in God's image (Genesis 1:26–27). Therefore, each one of us is created to be a creator! Perhaps it would be more theologically precise to say we are co-creators. But the point remains the same: God wants us to live our lives in creative ways that make beautiful art that fills the cosmos with praise and resounds to his glory.

You don't need to paint a masterpiece that is displayed in a museum in order to live a life of God-honoring creativity. One person who understood this well was Edith Schaeffer, the wife of Francis Schaeffer. In her book *Hidden Art*, she argues:

Man was created that he might create. It is not a waste of man's time to be creative. It is not a waste to pursue artistic or scientific pursuits in creativity, because this is what man was *made* to be able to do.

Over the course of fourteen chapters, Schaeffer describes what we might call "everyday creativity" and encourages each one of us to embrace activities like interior decorating, gardening, flower arranging, cooking, enjoying recreation, choosing clothing, and having an approach to the environment that reflects the fact that we have been created in the image of God, the Ultimate Creator.

John Donne—or at least Dr. John Donne—understood these things. His growth and evolution—from the passionate fires of youth, to the challenges of adulthood, and to the onset of illness and death—reveal him to be a person who allowed God to craft him into the kind of instrument he could use to make beautiful music.

Will you allow God to do the same with you? And will you work to approach everything in your life with a sense of God-given creativity? This is my prayer for you.

LEARNING MORE ABOUT
John Donne and England's Metaphysical Poets

Donne's poetry is available in many collections and anthologies. We have relied most heavily on two sources: the Penguin paperback volume, *John Donne: The Complete English Poems* (1973), and the ever-reliable *Norton Anthology of English Literature*, Vol. 1 (1974), which also includes a few poems by Herbert and Traherne.

Donne's work as a preacher and prose stylist finally gets the overdue attention it deserves in *One Equal Light: An Anthology of the Writings of John Donne*, compiled by John Moses (Eerdmans, 2004).

Donne scholarship is a growth industry, and the range of biographical and critical material is so vast that we hesitate to become enmeshed in bibliographic battles. But we can recommend the excellent study, *John Donne: Man of Flesh and Spirit* (Eerdmans, 2001). The book, which treats Donne's work as a poet and a preacher with equal respect, is written by Anglican cleric and scholar David L. Edwards, who says, "I believe that this is the first book about Donne ever to have been written by a man who has preached often in London, as he did."

Wonderful brief portraits of Donne, Herbert, and Traherne can be found in Richard H. Schmidt's eminently readable book, *Glorious Companions: Five Centuries of Anglican Spirituality* (Eerdmans, 2002).

For greater insight about how to apply your God-given creativity to every aspect of your life, track down a copy of Edith Schaeffer's *Hidden Art* (Tyndale, 1971). It will probably be easier to locate copies of Julia Cameron's best-selling *The Artist's Way: A Spiritual Path to Higher Creativity* (Tarcher, 1992), which contains general spiritual insights that can be readily used by people of many faiths. My own short book, *The Master Musician* (Zondervan, 1992), covers similar territory from my perspective as a Catholic Christian musician. The book is a companion project to the musical recording of the same name.

The Way of the Inner Light

George Fox

George Fox was a radical man who lived in radical times, and when I think about his life I am often reminded of the 1960s—a turbulent decade that contained more than its share of rebellion, revolution, and radical critiques of the status quo. For me and for millions of people like me, this was a time of searching questions and deep change.

A battle cry arose across the globe, as young people declared that new times demanded new approaches and that if members of the establishment didn't like it, they could just get lost.

Student protesters marched against war or attacked university leaders they considered out of touch. Young men and women explored new ways of relating to each other that flaunted traditional moral codes. And people of all kinds seem to lose faith in institutions, whether they were political, corporate, or religious.

It's certainly easy to make fun of the sixties, which had more than their share of silliness and unbridled excess. But this was also a time when many people embarked upon a passionate, no-holds-barred quest for spiritual truth.

I read George Fox's *Journals* many times during my own spiritual pilgrimage. At the time, I was becoming more and more intrigued by the life and teaching of Jesus, and I was struck by some of the parallels between the ministry of Christ and Fox's amazing experiences during the early years of the Quaker church.

Fox and other early Quakers were mystics, and as I read some of the accounts of their experiences, it seemed as though I was reading the stories of the early church in the New Testament Book of

Acts all over again. Fox wasn't the first person who tried to return to the pure and simple values of the New Testament, and he certainly wouldn't be the last. But as I learned more about his faith and his struggles, the Bible somehow became new and fresh and powerful for me. And as I read about the Quaker's profound spiritual experiences, I suddenly realized that something vital was missing from the Methodist and Baptist churches I was attending in my desperate attempt to find a church home.

Another thing that struck me about Fox and the early Quakers was their dedication to simple living. St. Francis had emphasized gospel simplicity in the thirteenth century. These ideas would influence Anabaptist, Mennonite, and Amish communities of the seventeenth and eighteenth centuries and even Utopian communities of the nineteenth century.

I was familiar with some of the many hippie communes that sprang up in the 1960s. Some were based on Eastern or New Age philosophies; others subscribed to Christian beliefs. As I looked around me at so-called mainstream American Christianity, I saw that most people preferred their lives of suburban consumption to the radical approach of the first Christians who shared everything they owned with fellow believers. As far as I could tell, Fox and the Quakers were on the side of simplicity, and that made me like them even more.

One of the best-known Quakers of our day is writer Richard Foster, whose best-selling *Celebration of Discipline* has had a profound impact on the spiritual lives of many people. Here's what Foster says about Fox:

> He was a bold and passionate man who acted with the certainty
> of one who knows God firsthand, not by hearsay. He was quick to
> confront those who "did not possess what they professed." He laid
> bare pomposity and pretense. He also called thousands to a direct,
> intimate knowledge of Christ, who was present to teach and
> empower them.

How did Fox and his followers develop their radical views? In order to understand this, we will have to travel back in time to seventeenth-century England.

A Culture of Chaos

Wracked by upheaval and uncertainty, George Fox's seventeenth-century England was a far cry from the "Merrie Olde England" of popular imagination. There were plots against the government, civil wars that pitted brother against brother, violent labor demonstrations that questioned centuries-old class structures, widespread rejection of church authority in any form, and a rapid growth in religious sects and cults—some of which taught that the end of the world was imminent.

Things were so crazy and chaotic that end-times doomsday scenarios didn't seem all that farfetched. And in the face of such turmoil, just about everyone seemed to be asking who made the rules, why they mattered, and whether or not they should be obeyed.

As for Fox, his spiritual goals were both simple and revolutionary. "Oh therefore you who know the light, walk in the light," he sometimes yelled at the top of his lungs to anyone who would listen, "for there are children of darkness that will talk of the light and the truth and not walk in it."

Preaching to the people of the Leicestershire area where he grew up, Fox boldly announced his mission:

> [It was] to bring people off their old ways . . . from their churches . . . from all the world's religions . . . from all the world's fellowships, and prayings, and singings . . . from heathenish fables, and from men's inventions and windy doctrines . . . and all their images and crosses, and sprinkling of infants, with all their holy days . . . and all their vain traditions.

Stretching Martin Luther's idea of the "priesthood of all believers" in ways that many Protestants and Catholics considered excessive, Fox was a radical mystic who turned his back on friends, family members, and churches to focus himself more fully on something he considered the only truly reliable source of inner illumination. He called this source the "Inner Light of the Living Christ."

Energized by that light, Fox traveled throughout the world, proclaiming a new gospel and a new era for the church. William Penn, one of his earliest and most influential followers, remembers him as a unique man who was uniquely called. "God sent him," wrote Penn, who would later found a Quaker-style New World colony called Pennsylvania. "As to man he was an original, being no man's copy."

Others remember Fox as a tireless preacher, a mesmerizing speaker, a natural promoter, and a skilled organizer. And before he knew it, this self-styled reformer became the father of a growing international movement called "Children of the Light" or "Friends of Truth," which would later become known as the Society of Friends.

Today, most of us are more familiar with the group's nickname: Quakers. Originally intended as an insult by one of the many judges who convicted Fox of blasphemy and threw him in a dirty jail cell, the term accurately described the fervor of some of the group's original gatherings, where both men and women were free to share their spiritual insights, and worshippers demonstrated their willingness to "tremble at the word of the Lord."

A Solitary Soul

Drayton-in-the-Clay was a little out-of-the-way town, but like the rest of England it was undergoing rapid change. The Glorious Revolution had declared Parliament (not the king) as the nation's ultimate authority. Low-paid workers were demanding their rights and winning concessions from the landed gentry. New "Radical Reformation" groups like the Mennonites, the Swiss Brethren, and the Hutterites sought members and respectability. And men like

Christopher Fox—a local weaver—were demanding the freedom to worship however they pleased.

Mr. Fox—a man so stern and zealous that neighbors called him a "Righteous Christer"—passed much of his rugged individualism on to his only son, George—a pious boy who had few friends. George would later describe himself in his own *Journal*, which was published three years after his death, this way: "In my very young years I had a gravity and staidness of mind and spirit not usual in children."

As a young man, George drank from what he called "the cup of fornication." He never gave any details about what his indiscretions might have been, and since this was centuries before twenty-four-hour cable news channels and rumor-filled Web sites, the details were never revealed. He also received a hefty inheritance from his parents that made him financially secure, if not wealthy. Sex and money might have seduced other lads, but they failed to dampen Fox's spiritual passion, which led him to pack his Bible and a few personal belongings in a bag and walk out of town, leaving behind everything he had ever known to begin his own quest for spiritual enlightenment.

"Thou seest," he wrote, "how young people go together into vanity and old people into the earth; and thou must forsake all, both young and old, and keep out of all, and be as a stranger to all."

It was 1643. Fox was nineteen years old. And the object of his quest was a Christianity that was true and pure and uncorrupted by powerful popes, grasping kings, and self-serving preachers.

Wearing rough leather clothes and a large leather hat, Fox traveled from town to town, sleeping in inns when he could or out in the fields when he had to. Like some hippies from the 1960s, he wasn't overly concerned about superficial matters like bathing, grooming, or following conventions of social etiquette. All he cared about was discovering the truth that would lead to inner transformation, and if people didn't like that they could just get lost.

George Fox and His Time

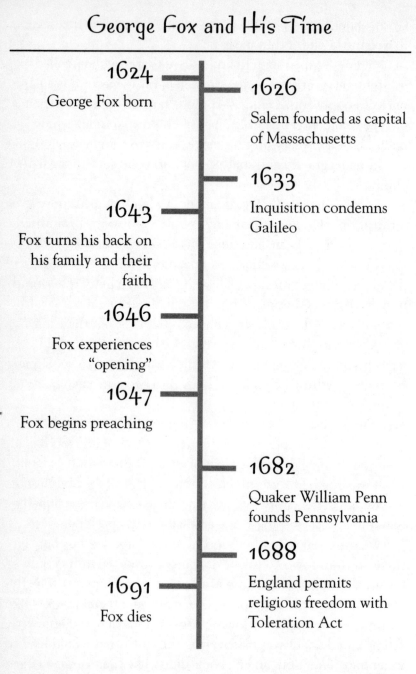

1624

George Fox born

1626

Salem founded as capital
of Massachusetts

1633

Inquisition condemns
Galileo

1643

Fox turns his back on
his family and their
faith

1646

Fox experiences
"opening"

1647

Fox begins preaching

1682

Quaker William Penn
founds Pennsylvania

1688

England permits
religious freedom with
Toleration Act

1691

Fox dies

He didn't get much help from priests or clergymen. "I saw they were all miserable comforters," he wrote. One time he walked seven miles to interview a priest who had a reputation for wisdom, but the exercise was a disappointment, and Fox dismissed the priest as a hypocrite. "I found him only like an empty hollow cask."

Then one day Fox had one of the first of the many mystical experiences he would call "openings." It came to him as he walked near the town of Coventry. It was a Sunday morning in the year 1646. Most people were in church, but Fox didn't think that was where God could be found. He described the occasion in his *Journal*.

> The Lord opened unto me "that being bred at Oxford or Cambridge was not enough to fit and qualify men to be ministers of Christ"; and I wondered at it, because it was the common belief of the people. But I saw it clearly as the Lord opened it to me, and was satisfied, and admitted the goodness of the Lord who had opened this thing unto me that morning.

Fox mentioned his revelation to his parents, but they were unimpressed and never lent their son any support.

> My relations were much troubled that I would not go with them to hear the priest; for I would get into the orchards, or the fields, with my Bible, by myself. . . . I saw that to be a true believer was another thing than they looked upon it to be.

As for the other Protestant religious groups that had multiplied like rabbits in the century since Luther's reforms, Fox felt they were all equally misguided. A newer and more radical approach was needed. "So neither these, nor any of the Dissenting people, could I join with, but was a stranger to all, relying wholly upon the Lord Jesus Christ."

Igniting a Fire

If Fox had remained "a stranger to all" there would have been no Quaker movement. But he couldn't keep quiet about the amazing things he was learning in his openings. "I was sent to turn people from darkness to the light," he announced.

Fox would typically enter a town, find lodging at an inn, and begin striking up conversations with those "tender souls" he perceived might be open to his message. On market days, he would speak to larger groups of farmers and merchants, occasionally climbing atop the large cross that could be found in the center of most market towns. On other occasions, he would sit perched atop a large haystack and wait for a suitable audience to gather.

The settings varied, but the message did not. "I showed them that God was come to teach his people by his Spirit, and to bring them off from all their old ways, religions, churches, and worships."

Fox had intense eyes, and there were times when he would fix his gaze on one person until he or she fell to the floor. He would grab people by the hand or the arm as he preached, squeezing their limbs in his vise-like grip as he emphasized a point. Before long, the spark of his zeal ignited a flame that burned throughout the English midlands. Or as Richard Farnworth, an overexcited disciple, put it, "The world is all on fire."

Both Fox and his followers began to compare his ministry to that of Christ, and there were numerous accounts of miracles and healings accompanying his preaching, just as such supernatural confirmations had accompanied the preaching of the Apostles in the earliest days of the church.

Not all his hearers welcomed Fox's radical message. During one meeting, a man approached Fox, striking his arm with a heavy wooden beam. The arm should have broken, but it remained unharmed, and instead the thick beam broke in two. Everyone was amazed, most of all Fox himself. After the meeting, the attacker approached him again. Fox raised his hand and beseeched the man to stay away, explaining that the supernatural protection provided by the Holy Spirit during the meeting was now gone, which meant any subsequent attack would leave his body badly injured.

Those who questioned Fox's claims of divine sustenance were hard-pressed to explain where he got his boundless energy. He was relentless in his pursuit of new disciples and ruthless in the way he treated his body. He slept little, ate less, passed the night in wet fields, and traveled tirelessly on foot and on horseback throughout England. When he sensed his work in one town was complete, he would sling his few belongings on his back and set off for the next town. And as his fame grew, he was accompanied by a growing but ragtag band of disciples.

Before long, Fox began portraying himself as a modern messiah. He told his host at one alehouse that he was "the son of God." Later on, when he began writing epistles to his far-flung followers, he would remind them that his words came not from his own mind but "from the authority of the Church in England, the pillar and ground of truth, [of] whom Christ is the head."

Using images of fire and brimstone, he warned one group of listeners: "The mighty day of the Lord is come. Every one who does not hear this prophet is to be cut off."

Fox's *Journal* is full of stories showing the tragic events that befell those who opposed God's prophet or his followers. One "evil-minded man" came to arrest Fox, but he "fell off his horse, and broke his neck. So there was a wretched end of a wicked informer." A separate *Journal* entry tells of "another of those rude butchers, who had sworn to kill me, having accustomed himself to thrust his tongue out of his mouth, in derision of Friends, when they passed by him, had it so swollen out of his mouth, that he could never draw it in again, but died so."

A Spiritual Lone Ranger

George Fox was no great fan of Catholics, but there were times when the openings he described in his *Journal* sounded an awful lot like the experiences Catholic mystics had undergone.

In one case, Fox described being "ravished with the sense of the love of God." On another occasion he said, "Whilst I was under spiritual suffering, the state of the New Jerusalem, which comes down out of heaven, was opened to me." This vision of paradise transformed his senses. "All things were new; and all the creation gave another smell unto me than before, beyond what words can utter." And he was often moved by the power of God's love. "At another time, I saw the great love of God, and I was filled with admiration of the infinitude of it. . . . I was wrapped up in the love of God, so that I could not but admire the greatness of his love."

But there were important differences between Fox and the many mystics who preceded him. Perhaps the most distinctive characteristic of Fox's spirituality was his all-out antiauthoritarian approach toward Christian tradition, the churches of his day, or anyone else who criticized or questioned his conclusions.

From the time of the Desert Fathers, many mystics were members of monasteries, drawing comfort and guidance from others in their communities. Fox was a spiritual Lone Ranger who didn't think he needed any outside assistance. "The Lord would teach the people himself," he said.

Where Luther had proclaimed his doctrine of the priesthood of all believers, Fox seemed to advocate the priesthood of the *solitary* believer. He held all churches—Catholic and Protestant—in contempt. He explained why in his *Journal*:

> At another time it was opened in me, "That God, who made the world, did not dwell in temples made with hands." This at first seemed strange. . . . But the Lord showed me clearly, that he did not dwell in these temples which men had commanded and set up, but in people's hearts. . . . His people were his temple, and he dwelt in them.

Fox wouldn't even dignify houses of worship by calling them churches. Instead he called them "steeple houses."

Fox also believed his inner revelations were more reliable than those found in Scripture. Previous mystics like John of the Cross and Teresa of Avila relied on Scripture to critique and correct the impressions and insights they gained in their visions. Not Fox, who said his openings trumped all other authority. "When I had openings, they answered one another, and answered the Scriptures."

Fox even said that only those who were properly illumined could understand Scripture's many mysteries. "I saw plainly that none could read Moses aright, without Moses' spirit." He criticized many people for trying to read the Bible in a "fleshly" manner. "They that had the Scriptures, but not the Spirit that gave them forth, come not to the life," he said.

Baptists, among others, were quick to dish out their own critiques of Fox, condemning him for relying solely on "a God within, and a Christ within, and a word within."

Biographer H. Larry Ingle's 1994 book, *First Among Friends: George Fox and the Creation of Quakerism*, provides a thorough look at some of the theological controversies that dogged Fox throughout his life. For example, critics were infuriated by Fox's claims that he and his followers could achieve a state of sinless perfection similar to "that state in which Adam was before he fell."

In this and many other cases, Fox went his own way and seemed unconcerned that some of his doctrines differed with centuries' worth of Christian orthodoxy. As Ingle writes, "He did not stop to ask whether any of his ideas had been considered heretical ages ago, for his experience with God transcended in importance anything human beings could say or do about his views."

Militant Mystics

Many people were ready to embrace Fox's new gospel, and the more he traveled and preached his message, the larger his movement grew. Other church groups criticized the Quakers' theology, but nothing infuriated folks so much as Fox's confrontational tactics. Like hippies from the 1960s who burned their draft cards or ransacked college administration buildings, Fox was an in-your-face activist with a flair for the dramatic gesture, taking his condemnations of other churches into the churches themselves.

One of his most controversial tactics was to hijack Sunday morning church services. He would enter the congregation and stay seated until the Spirit moved him to stand up and condemn the pastor and all who followed him. In Beverly, an economically depressed town, Fox attacked the preacher for taking an exorbitant salary. "Come down, thou deceiver," he called out. "Mayest not thou blush for shame." In Lancaster, Quakers tacked flyers on the church doors, saying: "This is the idol's temple where the worship of beasts is upheld, down with it, down with it."

Fox condemned church bells, saying they were like market bells. The only difference was that religious wares were being peddled in churches. In Lichfield, Fox condemned the whole town ("Woe to the bloody city of Lichfield!"). When challenged to soften his approach, Fox could be ruthless. "Repent you swine and beast," he barked at one critic.

Understandably, such antics led to resentment and reprisals. In many cases, Fox's public preaching caused riots. There were dozens of times when he and his followers were attacked, beaten up, or chased out of town by angry, gun-wielding townspeople.

The Quakers' tactics also got them into trouble with the law. And appropriately enough, the first place Fox was arrested and jailed was at Nottingham—a town that three centuries earlier had been home to a tough-talking sheriff who had a run-in with a populist rabble-rouser by the name of Robin Hood. According to legend, Robin Hood stole from the rich and gave to the poor. And in a sense, Fox was a religious Robin Hood who undermined the authority of wealthy and established churches and empowered poor and often unschooled iconoclasts.

These efforts won him the approval of the huddled masses, but church and civic leaders clamped down hard, repeatedly arresting Fox and sentencing him to lengthy periods of confinement. But his growing trials and tribulations only strengthened his resolve and added to his powerful allure. After all, hadn't Jesus' Apostles been jailed? Hadn't the saints of old been persecuted for their faith?

Fox spent years in jail, but when he wasn't locked up he traveled around the world spreading the message of the Inner Light to Ireland, Europe, North America, and the West Indies. Today, there are nearly fifty thousand Friends in the United States and many thousands more throughout the world.

The early Quakers' many brushes with the law helped forge a deepening social conscience that would be one of the movement's most important legacies. More than 20,000 Quakers were fined or imprisoned in England for their faith, and more than 450 either were killed or died in prison. Prospects for religious freedom improved by the time England passed its Toleration Act of 1688. But as they endured the penalties enforced by a justice system they considered anything but just, the Quakers learned to apply the principles of their inner-directed faith to the harsh realities of the outside world (see sidebar).

A Solo Saint?

The Quaker movement grew rapidly in England, with regular meetings of Friends established throughout the country. Over time, the movement also formalized its teaching, much of it based on nearly five thousand epistles Fox wrote before his death. An administrative structure was also developed to oversee the movement and discipline those whose views differed from Fox's.

He was harsh with wayward Quakers, charging them with desiring a "false liberty, out of light, power, spirit, grace, truth, and the word of God." Such rebels, said Fox, were guilty of "evil designs," "obdurateness," "self-will," and "pernicious jealousies."

It seems ironic that Fox—a man who claimed his own inner enlightenment was superior even to Scripture—would be so harsh with any who differed with him. But he had to do something to rein in the radical individualism his movement had unleashed.

I've said before that much about George Fox and his times reminds me of the 1960s, but much about Fox also reminds me of myself. I was never a hippie, but I did come of age during the sixties. And along with my brother Terry, I traveled across the country with a country rock band that played at packed concerts with artists like the Grateful Dead, Jefferson Airplane, and Janis Joplin. This gave me an unusual perspective on the North American version of the countercultural youth movement that was growing so rapidly around the world.

Like any movement, the counterculture was a mixed bag. I appreciated the sincerity, authenticity, and spiritual hunger of many of the young people I saw. But I was less impressed by runaway sexual exploitation, widespread drug abuse and addiction, and the willingness of some people to follow virtually any crackpot spiritual guru who offered the promise of enlightenment.

Freedom was a core value of the sixties, but people had problems figuring out exactly how that important value would be applied to their lives. Did freedom mean a hungry person could freely "appropriate" a loaf of bread from a grocery store that was part of the evil capitalist "system"? Did that mean love was only truly free when it involved absolutely no obligations or commitments? Did freedom mean that spiritual liberation could come only through mindless enslavement to a totalitarian religious leader?

When I look at Fox, there's much I appreciate. It's important for people to go on religious quests that help them separate true religion from false. I believe it's also vitally important for each one of us to listen to God. And it's clear that God calls on certain individuals from time to time to shake things up in the church.

What worries me about Fox's mystical approach, though, is his insistence that enlightenment could come only to him, directly from God without any need for checking his new revelations against Biblical teaching and centuries of church tradition. Such over-reliance on untested revelations has been the cause of many schisms in the Quaker movement, both in Fox's day and in the centuries since.

There are also aspects of Fox's radical reforming zeal that worry me. I remember when I came to faith after my own mystical encounter with Christ in a Holiday Inn room where I was staying while on a Mason Proffitt tour. With the encouragement of some ex-hippies who had become self-described Jesus freaks, I scanned my New Testament looking for weapons I could use to hurl at establishment churches I believed had corrupted or compromised the truth of the gospel.

My first solo Christian recording, which was released in 1976, was full of my self-righteous indignation. In the song "How Long?" I sang about a coming tribulation that would engulf millions of people who were busily building their own private hell. And in "Would You Crucify Him?" I attacked members of the churchgoing establishment (I satirically called them "my religious friends") and charged them with numerous sins against Christ:

> So now I turn to you through your years of your robes and stained-glass windows
> Do you vainly echo your prayers "to please the Lord"?
> Profess the Marriage with your tongue, while your mind dreams like the harlot
> But if the Judge looks to your thoughts, can't you guess your reward?

I was an angry young believer back then, and I thought I had all the truth I needed on my own. And even though this was a very important period in my spiritual development, there came a time when I felt the need to submit to a community of believers that was bigger than me. This community included wise and mature followers of Christ who knew a thing or two about God that I hadn't learned yet.

Don't get me wrong. There is much about George Fox and the Quakers I respect. For example, many Friends practice a form of common prayer that is similar to contemplative forms of prayer that have been at the center of Christian mystical spirituality for centuries.

Friends worship services are also a breath of fresh air. Unlike many contemporary services, which are bright and noisy affairs, Friends meetings begin with a time of silence that continues until one of the members discerns the prompting of the Spirit to speak, offer a prayer, or start a song. This is a welcome alternative to contemporary services that are so given over to the spirit of secular gods like consumerism, entertainment, and celebrity that they come dangerously close to crowd manipulation.

I also appreciate the Quakers' commitment to a "charismatic" Christianity that allows the Holy Spirit to play a role in their lives and their corporate gatherings. They might not call themselves charismatics or even mystics, but they allow God to speak to them, and that's important.

Having said all this, I want to repeat a caution that has arisen throughout this chapter. Mystical experiences can be powerful, and we should all seek personal encounters with Christ. But at the same time, we should avoid getting so wrapped up in our own private

---

Friends of Truth and Justice

In 1947, the Nobel Peace Prize was awarded to two Quaker groups: the Friends Service Council of Britain and Ireland and the American Friends Service Committee. In providing aid to suffering people during and after World War II, these Quaker groups were carrying on a tradition of social justice started by George Fox and his followers three centuries earlier.

Fox was a committed nonconformist who opposed mandatory military service and the signing of loyalty oaths. On an even more basic level, Fox opposed social conventions that required inferiors to bow or remove their hats when in the presence of social superiors. Fox strongly believed in the equality of every person—both before God and in their dealings with one another. And his refusal to remove his own hat got him into hot water with many an angry judge.

Quakers were among the many Christians who were persecuted in England before religious toleration became the law of the land, and their sufferings solidified their commitment to religious freedom and social justice and their opposition to unjust sentences and the death penalty.

raptures that we become deluded and believe God has given us insights that are superior to those of everyone else. Other mystics in this book, like John of the Cross, did a much better job of testing their own personal revelations against Scripture (see "Testing the Spirits" section in "The Way of Darkness" chapter).

LEARNING MORE ABOUT
George Fox and the Quakers

Fox's *Journal* is available in many editions. The version we quoted from here was published in 1978 as part of the Doubleday Devotional Classics series.

> The passive resistance the Quakers exhibited inspired people like Gandhi and Martin Luther King Jr., and their deep commitment to social-justice work around the globe has inspired many, including me. For twenty years, I have worked closely with Mercy Corps—an international relief and development agency that serves the oppressed and the disenfranchised worldwide.
>
> George Fox was a bold defender of the weak and powerless, and his Quaker descendents have done much to both criticize and relieve the harmful inequalities that cause so much pain to so many in our world. This commitment to transforming the world is most relevant in a day when many so-called mystics give up their Christian responsibility in the world to focus exclusively (and even selfishly) on their own inner lives.
>
> Today, the Friends carry on the visionary work of their founder. The Friends World Committee for Consultation is an international organization that enjoys nongovernmental consultant status with the United Nations, and Friends work for peace and justice in some of the most troubled areas of the world.

Books about Fox have been written by Quaker loyalists, vehement anti-Quakers, and scholars whose perspectives cover some of the middle ground between these two extremes. Although some Quakers consider H. Larry Ingle's *First Among Friends: George Fox & the Creation of Quakerism* (Oxford, 1994) to be overly critical, we found it to be an invaluable guide to Fox's beliefs, work, and legacy.

Richard Foster briefly discusses Fox in two wonderful books: *Spiritual Classics* (HarperSanFrancisco, 2000) and *Streams of Living Water: Celebrating the Great Traditions of the Christian Faith* (HarperSanFrancisco, 1998).

Another popular contemporary Quaker writer is Philip Gulley, whose "Harmony" novels focus on the exploits of Pastor Sam Gardner of the Harmony Friends Meeting in Harmony, Indiana.

Finally, we must confess that we stole the phrase "priesthood of the *solitary* believer" from Baylor University theologian Ralph C. Wood, who used it in the pages of *Christianity Today* to describe the hyperindividualism of many modern evangelicals.

The Way of the Pilgrim

Lessons on Prayer from an Unknown Seeker

The Way of the Pilgrim—an unusual memoir of a unique and powerfully affecting spiritual journey that has inspired many readers since it was first printed in 1884—begins like this:

> By the grace of God I am a Christian man, by my actions a great sinner, and by calling a homeless wanderer of the humblest birth who roams from place to place. My worldly goods are a knapsack with some dried bread in it on my back, and in my breast pocket a Bible. And that is all.

The humble author doesn't bother telling us his name, and it's only when he is questioned by one of the many supporting actors who appear in his story that he reveals even the slightest details about his own life.

The author was a Russian man who lived during the mid-nineteenth century. He was born in a village near the town of Orel, which is some two hundred miles south of Moscow. His parents died when he was two, and along with an older brother he was adopted by devout and loving grandparents who took him to the Russian Orthodox Church and read the Bible with him at home.

Our author's brother was an angry boy who shoved him one day, causing a fall that resulted in a permanent disability. "I had lost the use of my left arm when quite a child," he writes. Then, when the two boys had grown into men, the angry brother went haywire. The grandparents had died, and it might have been fears about his inheritance that caused him to strike out like one of the crazed characters in Tolstoy or Dostoyevsky. Whatever the cause was, the brother stole our author's money and set his house on fire while he and his wife were sleeping inside. "We only just escaped by jumping out of a window in our nightclothes."

Just when you think things can't get any worse, they do. After two years of poverty and homelessness, the author's wife died. "I was now left entirely alone in the world," he writes.

He could have become depressed and withdrawn, forsaking his faith in God. Instead, he sought to draw closer to God, getting rid of everything he owned and launching out on a religious quest that would consume his life for more than a decade.

His quest was fueled by a Scripture reading he heard during liturgy one Sunday at the Orthodox Church. The reading came from the Apostle Paul's First Letter to the Thessalonians, but it was three simple words that grabbed our author's attention: "Pray without ceasing."

"It was this text," he writes, "more than any other, which forced itself upon my mind, and I began to think how it was possible to pray without ceasing, since a man has to concern himself with other things also in order to make a living."

This pious pilgrim's homeland and culture were much different from ours, but his concern is as urgent for us today as it was for him a century and a half ago. Expressed in its most simple form, that concern is this: How do I maintain a relationship with Jesus through constant prayer in the midst of a busy and demanding life full of obligations and dominated by a struggle for economic survival?

"What ought I to do?" he thought. "Where shall I find someone to explain it to me?" So he set out, following in the footsteps of countless pilgrims and hermits of earlier centuries who left the comforts and customs of home to devote all their time and energies to the ruthless and single-minded pursuit of God.

He spent years wandering through Russia and Siberia, traveling thousands of miles on foot as he went from one Christian shrine or monastery to another. At first, he was obsessed with his own need to find a spiritual teacher who could enlighten him. Then, after finding a wise and caring teacher, he continued his wanderings, sharing with others the many lessons he had learned along the way.

We can be thankful that our pilgrim wrote down his thoughts about the spiritual life and his observations about many of the people and places he encountered. Sooner or later he died, but we don't know where or when. Then somehow, his private journals (or a copy of them) mysteriously wound up in the hands of a Greek monk on Mount Athos—a holy mountain that is home to the most famous of the world's many Orthodox monasteries. This monk shared the journals with his brothers, some of whom requested copies of their own. Before long, the memoir was published under the original Russian title, *Candid Narratives of a Pilgrim to His Spiritual Father*.

Reading this classic book today, we can see that our author actually describes two overlapping pilgrimages: his physical journey to some of the Christian world's most sacred sites and his spiritual journey into a deeper relationship with God.

Our pilgrim's account of his travels and his reflections on what he learned along the way have influenced many people to embark on their own spiritual journey for God. His words have also encouraged others to view all of life as a kind of perpetual pilgrimage toward God. But even more important, his book has taught many how to practice a simple but powerful prayer called the Jesus Prayer that is still practiced today by believers all over the world. The lessons this pilgrim learned about prayer not only fulfilled his deepest spiritual longings but they continue to enlighten us today.

In Search of a Spiritual Master

The pilgrim began his quest for insight into prayer by visiting "churches where famous preachers are to be heard." The results were disappointing. "I heard a number of very fine sermons on prayer—what prayer is, how much we need it, and what its fruits are—but no one said how one could succeed in prayer."

Our pilgrim soon gave up on sermons. "I settled on another plan—by God's help to look for some experienced and skilled person who would give me in conversation that teaching about unceasing prayer which drew me so urgently."

The person our pilgrim was looking for was called a *starets*, or spiritual director, who in the Orthodox East is usually a monk, a hermit, or both. "The inward process could not go on properly and successfully without the guidance of a teacher," he wrote. Long common in Orthodox and Catholic traditions, spiritual directors have been virtually unknown in most Protestant circles until very recently. The tradition of spiritual directors goes back to the time of Jesus, who schooled twelve disciples over the course of three years in a personal, hands-on manner. Early Celtic Christian monks who lived together in pairs in humble huts called each other soul friends, with the older guiding the spiritual growth of the younger. Today's sacrament of confession has its roots in the ancient practice of spiritual direction.

Spiritual directors are also common in Eastern religions like Hinduism or Buddhism, where they are known as gurus or teachers. Although many people think of Christianity as a Western faith, it is actually a universal faith that has deep connections to both the East and the West—a fact that we will learn more about as we follow our pilgrim's journey.

As he explained his quest to those he met on the road, the pilgrim received many suggestions about wise holy men who might be able to help him. Unfortunately, none of these men seemed to have the particular insights he craved. "My failure to understand made me sad, and by way of comforting myself I read my Bible. In this way I followed the main road for five days."

In some ways, our pilgrim's quest reminds me of Quaker founder George Fox's hunger for spiritual insight. But whereas Fox ultimately rejected all human teachers in favor of a radically individualistic approach, our pilgrim continued looking for a spiritual director who would see his hunger for prayer as a divine gift and help him develop it.

He finally found the help he sought in a wise and compassionate old monk who warmly welcomed him. "Thank God, my dear brother, for having revealed to you this unappeasable desire for unceasing interior prayer," said the monk.

> Recognize in it the call of God, and calm yourself. . . . It has been granted to you to understand that the heavenly light of unceasing interior prayer is attained neither by the wisdom of this world, nor by the mere outward desire for knowledge, but that on the contrary it is found in poverty of spirit and in active experience in simplicity of heart.

That monk reached deep within his own heart and deep within the mystical tradition of Orthodox spirituality to find a jewel for our pilgrim. This jewel was an ancient prayer technique called the Jesus Prayer. Both simple and profound, the Jesus Prayer is a brief invocation that expresses the mystical soul of Eastern Christianity. As the monk explained:

> The continuous interior prayer of Jesus is a constant uninterrupted calling upon the divine name of Jesus with the lips, in the spirit, in the heart, while forming a mental picture of his constant presence, and imploring His grace, during every occupation, at all times, in all places, even during sleep.
>
> The [prayer] is couched in these terms, "Lord Jesus Christ, have mercy on me."

Praying the Jesus Prayer

The origins of the Jesus Prayer go back to the fourth or fifth century, and it remains a foundation of spiritual practice and monastic life today among Orthodox believers. When novice monks enter one of the Greek monasteries, reciting the Jesus Prayer is an important part of their private practice.

In its most ancient and simple form, the Jesus Prayer consisted of reciting the name of Jesus with each and every breath. This helped monks pray without ceasing, since they had to breathe to stay alive.

Later, this one-word prayer evolved into the Jesus Prayer the pilgrim was taught in Russia: "Lord Jesus Christ, Son of God, have mercy on me." Later still, some monks added the words, "a sinner," to the end of this prayer. It was thought that acknowledgment of sin was an important step for novice monks who might need to learn the lessons of repentance and conversion.

Even though it is a short and simple prayer, these nine words can become an avenue to deep theological reflection and growth. Each of the words in the prayer conveys important meanings. And as we meditate upon them over the course of many repetitions, these meanings become etched on our very hearts.

The term *lord*, at least for English speakers, comes from the old English word for feudal lords who could take the wheat of the farmers and turn it into bread. Spiritually, it signifies the One who can take the natural gifts and talents we offer him and can turn them into spiritual nourishment.

Jesus comes from the Hebrew word *Yeshua* (Joshua) and means savior or salvation. In order to really understand what it is to be saved, we have to appreciate what it means to be "lost" and then rescued by God. That's the meaning of the lines from the hymn, "Amazing Grace" ("I once was lost but now am found, was blind but now I see"). Today, those who have wrestled with addictions and received help through a 12-step program can also appreciate what it means to be lost and saved.

Christ means "anointed one." One hears much about "the anointing" in high-energy Pentecostal and charismatic churches, but anointing means much more than mere excitement. To be anointed by Christ's spirit means that our lives are empowered to become more like the life of Jesus in our own day and time. St. Paul says the spirit's work in our lives should produce "the fruit of the Spirit," and he identifies that fruit as "love, joy, peace, patience, kindness, goodness, faithfulness, gentleness, and self-control" (Galatians 5:22). By examining our lives and searching for signs of such spiritual fruit, we can begin to assess if we are truly anointed.

Son of God is a powerful term that conveys something of the divine mysteries of the Trinity and the Incarnation. Jesus is the eternally begotten Son of God within the Trinity for all eternity. He is, as the Nicene Creed states, "God from God, Light from Light, True God from True God. Eternally begotten, not made. One in Being with the Father." We regularly recite this ancient creed at our community, as do many Christians throughout the world. Christ also "emptied" himself through the mystery of the Incarnation. "For us, and for our salvation He came down from heaven, was born of the Virgin Mary, and became man," as the Apostles' Creed says. As we pray the words, "Son of God," we can meditate on these wonders.

"Have mercy on me" is rich in meaning. Mercy is not only forgiveness of sins but also deeply felt compassion. This speaks to the amazing love God has for us in Jesus Christ. No matter how far we have fallen, there is always a way back to God for those who long to return. This fills us with gratitude and love. It fills us with hope. When we cry out for mercy and know that our lives are in real need of the Savior's mercy, we are broken and humble and ready to ask for help in making a change for the better.

"A sinner" is already implied in the words about mercy, but "sinner" was added to provide additional benefit for beginners in the practice. "To sin" simply means to miss the mark of perfection that God has established. The word *sin* has even been used in archery tournaments to describe those many occasions when the arrow misses the bull's-eye. Most of us seek the things of God whether we know it or not. Most of us seek goodness and truth and beauty and love. But because we are not perfect, we do not normally hit the bull's-eye. Therefore, our life is off center. It is off kilter, like an out-of-balance tire on an Ozark mountain highway that could become dangerous and harmful to life and limb if it is not set right. Sin is equally dangerous, and by acknowledging our sin to God, we invite his forgiveness and grace.

This is merely a brief outline of the deep theological meanings we can encounter through the eight simple words of the Jesus Prayer. But in order for the prayer to have its full effect, we should go beyond mere meaning and seek to understand the prayer mystically.

Each time we pray the prayer, we should seek to grasp its meaning, not only with the mind but also intuitively. In fact, trying to mentally grasp the meaning of each word of the prayer as we pray it would be mentally confusing. This would be a distraction from prayer. Rather, the full meaning of the Jesus Prayer is best grasped when intuited on the level of spirit beyond the senses, the emotions, or the mind. Then it can do the deeper work of salvation that will ultimately affect all the other areas for the better as well.

And as our pilgrim was about to find out, his spiritual director would seek to teach him some of these deeper realities of this deceptively simple prayer.

A Journey into the Heart of God

After teaching the pilgrim the Jesus Prayer, the old monk told him to go pray and report back to him. When our pilgrim returned for his first report, his wise spiritual director began guiding his development. "You ought from today onward to carry out my directions with confidence," he said, "and repeat the prayer of Jesus as often as possible. Here is a rosary. Take it and to start with say the prayer three thousand times a day."

The pilgrim found the assignment difficult at first, but it soon became "easy and likeable." He reported back to his spiritual director, who commanded that he now say the prayer six thousand times a day.

Taking no notice of any other thoughts however much they assailed me, I had but one object, to carry out my starets's bidding exactly.

And what happened? I grew so used to my prayer than when I stopped for a single moment I felt, so to speak, as though something were missing.

After ten days, the pilgrim visited the spiritual director again. This time, he was commanded to say the prayer twelve thousand times a day—a rate that would require the pilgrim to say the prayer about once every seven seconds.

The pilgrim decided to devote an entire summer to mastering the Jesus Prayer, taking up residence in a small hut he had adopted as his temporary home. By day two, the pilgrim was praying up a storm. His only problems were numbness in his tongue, a dull pain in the roof of his mouth, and an inflammation of his thumb and wrist from counting out his prayers on his rosary beads.

Then before he knew what was happening, the pilgrim felt that he was no longer praying the prayer. Instead, the prayer was praying *him*. "Early one morning the prayer woke me up as it were," he writes. "I felt as if I was cut off from everything else." Our pilgrim soon discovered that saying the prayer had transformed his life.

> My mind tended to listen to it, and my heart began of itself to feel at times a certain warmth and pleasure. . . . My lonely hut seemed like a splendid palace, and I knew not how to thank God for having sent to me, a lost sinner, so wholesome a guide and master.

Having mastered the prayer, our pilgrim finally bid farewell to his beloved spiritual director and continued his journey. But this pilgrimage seemed different from his initial wanderings. "Now I did not walk along as before, filled with care. The calling upon the name of Jesus Christ gladdened my way. Everybody was kind to me; it was as though everyone loved me."

Well, not exactly everyone. Our pilgrim was knocked unconscious and his knapsack stolen by a pair of roving robbers. But he viewed the incident as a lesson in detachment taught by a loving God and continued along his way. As he did so, the prayer grew more deeply in his heart.

> The prayer had, so to speak, by its own action passed from my lips to my heart. That is to say, it seemed as though my heart in its ordinary beating began to say the words of the prayer within at each beat. . . . I gave up saying the prayer with my lips. I simply listened carefully to what my heart was saying.

With each additional step, the pilgrim found new glories to behold. The Scriptures opened up their wisdom to him as he meditated on various passages. Even the creation bore witness to the majesty and beauty of the Creator.

"Everything around me seemed delightful and marvelous," he wrote. "All things prayed to God and sang his praise. . . . Everything drew me to love and thank God: people, trees, plants, and animals. . . . I saw clearly all my internal organs and was filled with wonder at the wisdom with which the human body is made."

As he traveled, our pilgrim shared the insights he had gained with anyone who would listen. And even though it had been more than a decade since his heartfelt desire to "pray without ceasing" had first caused him to hit the road, that desire continued to animate him and guide his contacts with others. As he told one of the many people he met along the way, "In short, let every action be a cause of your remembering and praising God."

Praying with Mind and Heart and Breath

As he traveled, our pilgrim studied his Bible, as well as a book called *The Philokalia* that his spiritual director had given him. *The Philokalia* (the title means "Love of what is beautiful") is an eighteenth-century collection of mystical and ascetic writings, most of which were written by Eastern Christian preachers and monks between the fourth and fifteenth centuries.

The Philokalia deals with many subjects, including the Jesus Prayer, but it places this prayer in a broader context of "breath prayers" that are part of an ancient mystical approach called Hesychasm, a tradition of inner, mystical prayer associated with the

Orthodox monks of Greece's Mt. Athos. The breath prayers of the Hesychast mystics seek to unite body and spirit in prayer.

When those of us who live in the West hear someone talking about uniting body and spirit, we assume they are endorsing an "alternative" approach that has its roots in the religions of the East or in Eastern religious principles that have been popularized in the so-called New Age movement. But breath prayers have been at the center of Christian spiritual practices in the East for centuries.

As our pilgrim traveled throughout Russia, he ran into many people who were skeptical about the Jesus Prayer's origins. But he set them straight, tracing its lineage from Christian saints like Antony of the Desert, John Chrysostom, and others. "It was from them that the monks of India . . . took over the 'heart method' of interior prayer," he said—not the other way around.

The Christian concept of breath prayer comes from *ruah*, the Hebrew word for spirit, which refers to both the "wind" and the "intimate breath" of God. Jesus said that the Spirit of God is like the wind (John 3:8), and the Book of Acts reports that when the Holy Spirit descended on the Apostles on the Day of Pentecost, it was accompanied by "a sound like the blowing of a violent wind" (Acts 2:2).

Like our pilgrim, monks and mystics of the Christian East found that uniting their prayers with their breathing could help them fulfill Paul's admonition to "pray without ceasing," since we must breathe to stay alive. Uniting the prayer with the breath was also a way to pray in the power of the Spirit of God. They found that uniting the breath with the repetition of the name of Jesus enabled them to pray in the name of Jesus intuitively, beyond concepts or words. Over time, this simple prayer developed into the formal Jesus Prayer that was taught to our pilgrim.

Medical research has shown that breath prayer produces certain physiological effects, no matter what faith a person follows. Measured breathing slows down the body, the emotions, and the thoughts, making it easier to focus the meditation and decreasing annoying distractions.

For the Christian, breath prayer does much more than this. It unites us with Jesus in the Spirit of God. It focuses our thoughts and emotions on the character of God. And as mystics have realized for centuries, it gets us in touch with the concept of Christian poverty by helping us contemplate those very basic functions that keep us all alive. And as our pilgrim discovered, after the formal prayer is learned and mastered, it teaches us to pray intuitively and continually with each and every breath we breathe.

How can you learn to practice breath prayers like the Jesus Prayer? I have learned some techniques and practices over the years that might help you.

Learning to Breathe

When I teach on the Jesus Prayer or, more generally, on breath prayer, I stress that you must first find a quiet place that will be relatively free from intrusion during your meditation time. Next, you must adopt a bodily posture that will enable you to stay relatively still and quiet for twenty to thirty minutes.

There has been much debate about what is the best bodily posture. Some adopt a traditional cross-legged position. Others find that sitting in a straight-backed chair, with feet flat on the ground and head and shoulders lined up straight, is a stable and comfortable posture. There is no best posture for everyone. You must find the posture that works best for you.

You might want to rest your hands in your lap or give them something to do that is minimal and restful, like fingering a stone or a rosary. Likewise, you may want to gently rest your tongue against the back of the front upper teeth on the upper palate. Keep your eyes slightly open, without focusing on any particular object. This will help you stay awake and keep you from getting distracted by items in your field of vision.

The first stage of practicing consists of simply learning to breathe deeply. As you breathe, picture your breath originating not in your nose but from your diaphragm, or navel. This is the way we breathe at night when we are sleeping, and it's the way infants breathe constantly. It is also the way we singers are taught to breathe while singing. Breathing from deep within relaxes the whole being but it also brings the greatest amount of oxygen to the lungs and blood, making us alert and healthy.

Next, as you continue breathing, take a mental inventory of your entire person, and let go of every aspect of yourself, trusting it to God through Christ. Start with your body and then continue through your emotions and thoughts. As you go through your inventory, simply acknowledge to God how you are doing today in the areas of body, emotions, and thoughts. Your reports may be positive or negative. But the important thing is to simply acknowledge each aspect of your life and release each aspect to God's loving care.

Next, try to recognize that you are a part of God's wonderful creation and interdependent with everything that exists. This awakens you to the wonder of your being, the wonder of God's creation, the wonder of Christ's Incarnation. It also generates a sense of gratitude for all God has made and done.

As you do so, try to recognize that all created things, including your body, are impermanent and transitory things that will pass away. Your emotions and your thoughts, as important as they seem, regularly rise and fall with the changing conditions of your life. As you meditate on this truth, let go of these things, and let them die through the cross of Jesus. By releasing everything temporal and transitory, in Christ you can grab hold of that which is eternal.

As you practice breath prayer daily for months and years, you will gradually find, just as our pilgrim did, a whole new person being reborn within you through the cross of Jesus Christ. It happens a day at a time, a breath at a time.

As you are freed from enslavement to your sensual appetites and the whirlwind of your disordered emotions and negative and confused thoughts, you will break through to the realm where your spirit comes into contact with God's Spirit. When that happens, you will begin to see all of life as a miracle of rebirth, awakening, and resurrection. This will lead you into a whole new way of thinking, feeling, and perceiving the reality in God.

Unleashing Your Own Inner Pilgrim

The world's major faith traditions have long described the religious life as an ongoing journey. Moses led the people of Israel through the deserts of the Middle East for forty years. Jesus had no place to lay his head. The Apostles traveled throughout the Mediterranean spreading the gospel. And Brendan the Navigator, one of the most famous Celtic monks, may have sailed his leather boat to North America nine centuries before Columbus came to the New World.

Christians have made pilgrimages to holy sites for centuries, but in recent years spiritual travel has been reborn, leading publishers to release dozens of new spiritually oriented guidebooks that devote equal attention to travel and transformation.

We live in an age when many people are so overworked they don't even take vacations. Many Americans do allow themselves a week or two of vacation every year, but thanks to high-tech devices like cell phones and palm computers, many workers are never more than a phone call or an e-mail message away from the demands of their work. As a result, many of those people who do take vacations never really "get away from it all."

But that's changing. As a *New York Times* columnist put it, "The travel in today's travel books has to be more than simply going from point to point: something more meaningful, sometimes even grander, always at least different." Jan-Erik Guerth, the editorial director for Paulist Press's The Spiritual Traveler series agrees. "Sacred journeys and sacred sites have been at the center of humankind's spiritual life from the very beginning," he says. "People are redefining and reinventing 'pilgrimage' for the 21st century."

San Francisco–based Travelers' Tales has published numerous spiritual travel guides, including *Pilgrimage: Adventures of the Spirit*, *A Woman's Path: Women's Best Spiritual Travel Writing*, and *The Road Within: True Stories of Transformation*. "We're all looking for ourselves, whether we know it or not," says editor Larry Habegger. "When we set out into the larger world we open ourselves up to the experiences of others, and automatically open our insides to a greater understanding of ourselves."

Other recent books focus on the spirituality of religious buildings. *Heaven in Stone and Glass: Experiencing the Spirituality of the Great Cathedrals* (Crossroad) is Robert Barron's moving meditation on the varied ways that the symbolic imagination of medieval architects led to the creation of some of the world's most majestic religious buildings. *Synagogues Without Jews* by Rivka and Ben-Zion Dorfman is a lovingly researched and lavishly illustrated look at deserted houses of worship in more than thirty small European cities and towns.

Many smaller publishers have also released state or regional guidebooks like *Colorado's Sanctuaries, Retreats, and Sacred Places*. Author Jean Torkelson, who works as the religion reporter for Denver's *Rocky Mountain News*, believes travel can help hard-charging, hectic people unwind, unburden themselves, and make vital spiritual connections.

"To me, if you come back from a vacation and are not spiritually renewed, what's the point?" says Torkelson. "Going to see Broadway shows or crashing on a beach can be great vacations, and they can renew you too, but it can be just as memorable and spiritually refreshing to find a small retreat house somewhere."

LEARNING MORE ABOUT
The Way of the Pilgrim

Like the anonymous author of *The Way of the Pilgrim*, we should think of our own journeys as taking place on two levels: the inner journey to God and the outward journey to sacred places where God has met his children in the past.

Unlike the other mystics featured in this book, the pilgrim's identity remains a mystery, which greatly reduces the number of books that can be written about him and his work. But that's OK. Our pilgrim's memoir is a classic account of the inner spiritual journey that needs little interpretation and remains surprisingly powerful today.

The edition we used combined both *The Way of the Pilgrim* and its less valuable sequel, *The Pilgrim Continues His Way*, both translated by R. M. French and originally published by HarperSanFrancisco in 1991. This book was repackaged as part of Quality Paperback Book Club's Mystical Classics of the World series in a 1998 edition, featuring a helpful introduction by renowned religion scholar Huston Smith. In addition, my album *Songs of Worship* (Vol. 2) features a song based on the Jesus Prayer.

As for the outer journey to sacred sites, many books will help you unleash your own inner pilgrim. Martin Robinson's *Sacred Places, Pilgrim Paths: An Anthology of Pilgrimage* (HarperCollins, 1997) is a very good place to start. Reference works include Robert Brockman's *Encyclopedia of Sacred Places* (Oxford, 1997) and Colin Wilson's *The Atlas of Holy Places & Sacred Sites* (DK, 1996).

Those interested in the Holy Land will appreciate Bruce Feiler's best-selling *Walking the Bible: A Journey by Land Through the Five Books of Moses* (Morrow, 2001). For Rome, see Frank Korn's *A Catholic's Guide to Rome* (Paulist, 2000). Kevin J. Wright's *A Pilgrim's Travel Guide* series (Ligouri) covers many areas of the world. One recent volume is devoted to *Europe's Monastery and Convent Guesthouses*. Steve and Lois Rabey's *Celtic Journeys: A Traveler's Guide to Ireland's Spiritual Legacy* (Citadel Press, 2001) explores

Celtic sites. And Zondervan's Christian Travelers Guide series includes volumes on Italy, France, Germany, and Great Britain.

Those traveling in America might appreciate Jay Copp's *The Ligouri Guide to Catholic U.S.A.* (1999) or Jack and Marcia Kelly's acclaimed Sanctuaries series of regional guides to monasteries, abbeys, and religious guesthouses across the United States.

The Way of Childlike Love
Thérèse of Lísieux

Even though they were enlisted in one of the most important projects in the history of our world, the twelve flawed men who accepted Jesus' call to be his disciples were often preoccupied with the most superficial kinds of squabbling and the most sophomoric forms of petty one-upmanship.

They demanded to know "who is greatest in the kingdom of heaven." They argued over who would sit at Jesus' right hand and his left hand when he began his eternal rule. They tried to trick and cajole him into declaring which one of them he considered the most committed to the cause or the most successful at effecting miraculous cures.

But unlike every other man who had ever lived, Jesus had no nagging insecurities about who he was, what he was supposed to do with his life, or how he measured up to others. So it's interesting to see how he handled his disciples' obsession with self-worth and social rank. One of his favorite ploys was to confound their haggling by focusing his attention on children. Matthew describes the time Jesus enlisted the help of a little child to serve as a living, breathing sermon illustration. He told his disciples this:

> I tell you the truth, unless you change and become like little children, you will never enter the kingdom of heaven. Therefore, whoever humbles himself like this child is the greatest in the kingdom of heaven. And whoever welcomes a little child like this in my name welcomes me [Matthew 18:3–5].

Mark records an equally interesting episode. As Jesus taught in a public place, people brought their children to him so he could touch them. The disciples considered this a huge waste of their master's precious time, so they rebuked the people. Mark tells us Jesus was indignant about his disciples' behavior, and he let them know all about it.

"Let the little children come to me," he said, "and do not hinder them, for the kingdom of God belongs to such as these. I tell you the truth, anyone who will not receive the kingdom of God like a little child will never enter it." Then Jesus took the children in his arms, put his hands on them, and blessed them (Mark 10:14–16).

Similar stories appear in Luke, as does this stinging rebuke of our belief that bigger is always better: "He who is least among you all—he is the greatest," Jesus told his disciples as they engaged in another of their frequent tiffs (Luke 9:48).

There are many times when I feel more like these sinful and self-centered disciples than I do some of the men and women featured in this book. Studying the lives and work of the great Christian mystics can be frustrating. Some of them appear to be spiritual giants who lived lives of perfect holiness and routinely enjoyed super-sized experiences that seem far beyond the grasp of normal mortals like ourselves.

That's why a simple, quiet, young French nun who died virtually unknown to anyone beyond a tiny circle of sisters only a century ago has rapidly become one of the world's most adored saints. Her name was Thérèse of Lisieux, and the legacy of her childlike faith and wholesome innocence is a much-needed antidote to the deadening cynicism we see in much of modern life. "The only way to make progress along the path of divine love is to remain very little and put all our trust in Almighty God," she said. "That is what I have done."

Thérèse, who was born in 1873 and died of tuberculosis in 1897 at the age of twenty-four, was an ordinary person transformed by an extraordinary love for God. By charting a "Little Way" to God that is open to anyone who truly desires a deeper spiritual life, she liberated sanctity, making it accessible to one and all:

> We live in a time of inventions. We need no longer climb laboriously up flights of stairs. And I am determined to find an elevator to carry me to Jesus, for I was too small to climb the steps of perfection.
>
> It is your arms, Jesus, which are the elevator to carry me to heaven. So there is no need for me to grow up. In fact: just the opposite: I must become less and less.

From Little Child to Little Flower

If there has ever been such a thing as a perfect childhood, the child named Marie-Francoise-Thérèse Martin had one. The youngest daughter of devout and devoted parents, Thérèse later recalled her childhood as a carefree time of domestic bliss.

> God was pleased . . . to surround me with love, and the first memories I have are stamped with smiles and the most tender caresses. But although he placed so much love near me, he also sent much love into my little heart, making it warm and affectionate.

Her Papa Louis was a watchmaker, and her Mamma Zélie was caring and nurturing. Both parents had unsuccessfully tried to enter monasteries when they were younger, and now they channeled all their bottled-up devotion into rearing their five surviving daughters, all of whom became nuns. Thérèse entertained her first notions of entering the religious life when she was two.

But tragedy invaded Thérèse's paradise with the death of her mother. Thérèse had once described the world as her private garden. "Oh! everything truly smiled upon me on this earth: I found flowers under each of my steps and my happy disposition contributed much to making life pleasant." But now her four-year-old heart was crushed.

206 THE WAY OF THE MYSTICS

> My happy disposition completely changed after Mamma's death. I, once so full of life, became timid and retiring, sensitive to an excessive degree. One look was enough to reduce me to tears, and the only way I was content was to be left alone completely.

Papa devoted himself even more completely to caring for his daughters during this painful time. "I wonder at times how you were able to raise me with so much love and tenderness without spoiling me," said Thérèse. But biographer John Beevers argues that she seriously underestimated how much she was pampered. "Thérèse was a thoroughly spoilt child and girl," writes Beevers, who is a sympathetic biographer. Other scholars say her doting father, her unusually close family ties, and the shock of her mother's death left her unusually timid and reclusive.

It was her blossoming love of God that gradually pulled her out of her downward cycle of grief and sadness. Often private about her encounters with God, Thérèse guardedly described her First Communion, which was a watershed moment in her life:

> I don't want to enter into detail here. There are certain things that lose their perfume as soon as they are exposed to the air; there are deep spiritual thoughts which cannot be expressed in human language without losing their intimate and heavenly meaning. [But] Ah! how sweet was that first kiss of Jesus.

That day, it was no longer simply a look; it was a fusion; they were no longer two. Thérèse had vanished, as a drop of water is lost in the immensity of the ocean.

Thérèse would shed many tears throughout her brief life, but from this time forward they were tears of a devoted lover who had an overwhelming sense of her own spiritual destiny. "I was born for glory," she wrote. "My own glory would not be evident to the eyes of mortals [but] would consist in becoming a great saint!"

When she was only fifteen, she entered the Carmelite monastery in Lisieux, where she adopted the name Thérèse of the Child

Jesus and the Holy Face. But in time, people would prefer to call her by another name: Little Flower. The name comes from a section of her autobiography where Thérèse describes herself as "the *little flower* gathered by Jesus."

Thérèse saw all creation as a garden tended by God, and she saw people as flowers in that garden. Building on this simple metaphor, she explored the conundrum of "why all souls don't receive an equal amount of graces." As she saw things, the Divine Gardener appreciated the unique beauty of each and every one of his many varied flowers.

"The splendor of the rose and the whiteness of the lily do not take away the perfume of the little violet or the delightful simplicity of the daisy," she said.

> And so it is in the world of souls, Jesus' garden. He willed to create great souls comparable to Lilies and roses, but He has created smaller ones and these must be content to be daisies or violets destined to give joy to God's glances when He looks down at His feet. Perfection consists in doing His will, in being what He wills us to be.

From Little Flower to Mega-Saint

Thérèse was a quiet woman who was perfectly content to grow where God planted her. The only time she ever traveled any distance was when she went on a pilgrimage to Rome the year before she entered the cloister. She rarely left the monastery, which was located a short walk from her home, and she had little contact with the outside world. During her brief life, only a few people knew her, including her two-dozen fellow sisters, a handful of family members, and a few local children who attended an abbey school with her.

Thérèse had said that her glory would not be evident to human eyes, but she was dead wrong about that, for her popularity grew like a brush fire in a parched land.

Her older sister Pauline had entered the monastery first, and it was she who commanded Thérèse to write her life story. When the

Thérèse and Her Time

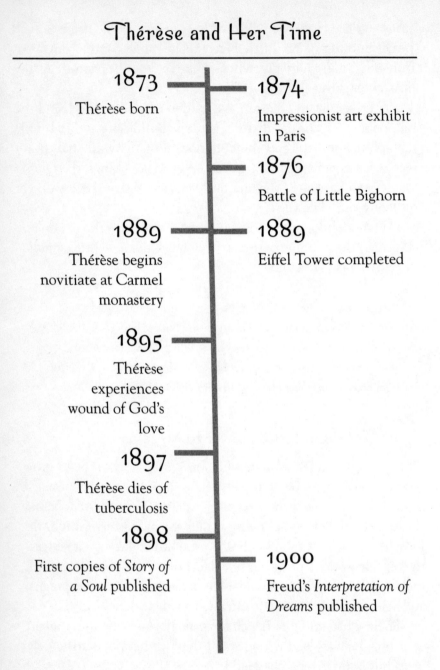

1873
Thérèse born

1874
Impressionist art exhibit in Paris

1876
Battle of Little Bighorn

1889
Thérèse begins novitiate at Carmel monastery

1889
Eiffel Tower completed

1895
Thérèse experiences wound of God's love

1897
Thérèse dies of tuberculosis

1898
First copies of *Story of a Soul* published

1900
Freud's *Interpretation of Dreams* published

first two thousand copies of *Story of a Soul* were published in 1898—one year after her death—one of the sisters at the monastery asked, "How are we going to dispose of all these?" But that proved to be no problem.

Within a decade, *Story of a Soul* had been translated into English, Italian, Dutch, German, Polish, and Portuguese. Within twenty years, it had sold more than 200,000 copies, and an abridged version had sold 700,000 copies. By this time, the sisters had also distributed 800,000 photos of the young nun with the Mona Lisa smile, as well as more than a million sachets, or small envelopes of silk, containing scraps of material she had touched. Before long, every single sheet, curtain, or article of clothing Thérèse had ever come in contact with was gone. But that didn't stop people from writing the monastery, which received hundreds of letters a day.

In the face of such popular piety, the Vatican put the investigation into Thérèse's possible canonization on the fast track. But the undistinguished nature of her life led many to doubt that she would be named a saint. "One never noticed anything extraordinary about her," one sister told a Vatican investigator. Another agreed, saying, "She has certainly never done anything worthy of speaking about."

Thérèse was named a saint in 1925, only twenty-eight years after her death—a pace that's unprecedented in church history. At the huge Vatican ceremony celebrating her canonization, Pope Pius X read Jesus' words about the faith of a child. In 1997, the one hundredth anniversary of her death, she was named a Doctor of the Church. She was only the third woman to receive this honor.

That year also marked the beginning of a worldwide tour of the saint's relics (or bones) that traveled around the world in a four-hundred-pound coffin-like reliquary. When the relics arrived in Detroit, some twenty thousand people came to view them. And crowds lining up to see the relics at New York's St. Patrick's Cathedral stopped traffic on Fifth Avenue. But such turnouts were small compared to the reception Thérèse received in Ireland. Over a period of seventy-eight days in 2001, an estimated three million people (or about three-fourths of the nation's population) turned out to pay their respects.

She has been the subject of hundreds of biographies (including one written by Catholic activist Dorothy Day), numerous films (including a 1986 movie by French director Alain Cavalier), and numerous literary works (she shows up in novels by Graham Greene, Georges Bernanos, and others). She has played an important role in many women's decisions to enter the religious life, including my own wife, Viola. She has inspired thousands of parents to name their daughters Thérèse, and she is the namesake of the twentieth century's best-known nun, Mother Teresa of Calcutta.

So what made this quiet and unknown woman so popular so quickly? I believe it was her childlike love for God, the innocence of her faith, and her deep commitment to serving God. All of us are looking for models of sanctity we can grab hold of. We are looking for pioneers on the path of spiritual growth whose footsteps we can attempt to follow.

In the case of Thérèse, her proclamation of a Little Way to God made it seem that sainthood could be within reach of us all. Or as she put it, "Because I was little and weak He lowered Himself to me, and He instructed me secretly in the things of His love."

Unlocking a Soul

"I come to confide the story of my soul," writes Thérèse in the opening sentence of her autobiography. She claims she didn't want to write about herself but did so out of obedience.

The book remains the best key for unlocking the heart of this beloved saint and understanding her unique relationship to God and her sisters. And as Thomas Merton discovered, *Story of a Soul* reveals a mystical depth that seems surprising in a woman so young and so simple. Merton had once dismissed Thérèse as a spiritual lightweight but changed his tune after studying her more closely. "I owe her a profound apology," he said.

Thérèse's devotion to God was profound and all-consuming. "I loved God very much and offered my heart to Him very often," she wrote. Knowing that love was more than a feeling, she worked overtime to put her faith into action. "I understood that to become a saint one had to suffer much. . . . I cried out: 'My God, I choose all!' I don't want to be a saint by halves."

Thinking back on her childhood, she saw her nurturing home and devout upbringing as part of God's plan to protect her for Himself. "He forgave me *in advance* by preventing me from falling," she writes. "I have heard it said that one cannot meet a pure soul who loves more than a repentant soul; ah! how I would wish to give the lie to this statement!"

Her commitment to sanctity meant that her life would be a lonely one. She considered her friends too worldly ("They didn't think about death enough"), and she felt that no one could fathom her devotion to God.

> My heart, sensitive and affectionate as it was, would have easily surrendered had it found a heart capable of understanding it. I tried to make friends with little girls my own age . . . [but] my love was not understood.

But she knew she was not really alone after all. "God was already instructing me in secret," she says. "Jesus deigned to show me the road that leads to this Divine Furnace, and this road is the surrender of the little child who sleeps without fear in its Father's arms."

Thérèse received the habit of the Carmelite order in the spring of 1888. A light dusting of snow in the woods outside the monastery only heightened her sense of spiritual consummation. "Nature would be adorned in white just like me," she wrote. "What thoughtfulness on the part of Jesus!"

She embraced the order's harsh austerities, pushing herself much harder than any rules required. She also welcomed life in community as an opportunity to express her love of God through service to others. "My vocation is love," she wrote. "I applied myself to practicing little virtues, not having the capability of practicing the great."

Pen Pals and Soul Mates

His name was Maurice Belliere, and he was a struggling seminary student who wrote to the Carmelite monastery at Lisieux requesting that one of the sisters there pray for the salvation of his troubled soul.

"The grace of God which impelled me toward the Sanctuary has not washed away the last traces of a thoughtless life which preceded my decision," he wrote, "and in spite of my efforts I have a hard time absorbing the spirit of the Church and holding myself to all the demands of the seminary rule."

In time, Thérèse was asked to correspond with Maurice, and over the course of nearly two-dozen letters exchanged in the two years before her death, these pen pals became soul mates. "I feel our souls are made to understand each other," wrote Thérèse to Maurice, whom she affectionately called her "little brother."

Her letters provided unique comfort to Maurice—a troubled soul who endured a "disastrous" period of military service and was turned down by one missionary agency before being accepted by another. His letters were full of grumbling and regrets. "The missionary has to be a saint, and a saint I am not," he wrote.

Thérèse tried to communicate grace and encouragement to Maurice. "When Jesus calls a person to lead a great number of others to salvation, it is very necessary that He make him experience the trials and temptations of life," she wrote in one letter. In another, she discussed perseverance in the midst of suffering. "Your lot is truly beautiful, since Our Lord chose it for Himself and first put His own lips to the cup which He now holds to yours."

Maurice deeply appreciated Thérèse's letters. "One breathes in from [them] a divine inspiration which makes one pure and strong."

As Thérèse felt her death approaching, she pledged to continue supporting Maurice once she had flown from the confines of the monastic life. "I promise to remain your little sister in heaven. Far from being broken, our union will become a closer one, for then there will be no more cloister and no more grills, and my soul will be free to fly with you to the missions far away." Then he asked,

> Do you realize that you open up new horizons to me? I have come to think the way you do, except that I possess only imperfectly that delightful simplicity . . . because I am a sad and conceited man, and I rely too much on created things. . . . I look upon everything you tell me as coming from Jesus Himself.

Maurice expressed his fears about losing his beloved sister and apologized for baring his soul in his letters. Thérèse reassured him: "It must be that you don't know me at all well, if you are afraid that a detailed account of your faults could lessen the tenderness that I feel for your soul!"

She wrote her final letter to Maurice just weeks before her death, sending along a crucifix she had possessed for a decade and the last of the many small religious paintings she had created. "I am now all ready to leave," she wrote. "I have my passport for heaven."

Maurice wrote right back: "Jesus is calling you. Go to God. . . . Go to feast your soul upon Love."

The years after Thérèse's death were tough on Maurice. He contracted sleeping sickness while serving as a missionary in Africa. The illness broke his health and his spirit, and he died in a mental hospital in 1907—a decade after he lost his beloved soul mate. He is buried outside a French church, and on the wall inside the church is a simple plaque that reads, "Maurice Belliere, Spiritual Brother And Protégé Of Saint Thérèse."

When she entered the monastery, Thérèse said her goal was to pray and to save souls. Her correspondence with Maurice indicates that she may have done both.

Committed to service and suffering, Thérèse made a habit of seeking out the most quarrelsome and unfriendly sisters. "I prefer vinegar to sugar," she said. "I must seek out . . . the company of the Sisters who are the least agreeable to me in order to carry out with regard to these wounded souls the office of the good Samaritan."

Such practices were a source of continual frustration for Thérèse, but she sought to rise above her frustrations with God's help. When one sister made an annoying clicking noise with her teeth, Thérèse tried to discern in it the sounds of "a delightful concert." A sister who worked with Thérèse in the laundry continually threw dirty water in her face. "I put forth all my efforts to desire receiving very much of this dirty water, and was so successful that in the end I had really taken a liking to this kind of aspersion." Thérèse committed to pray for another irritating sister. "Each time I met her I prayed to God for her, offering Him all her virtues and merits."

In someone other than Thérèse, such efforts might have yielded a bitter fruit of smug self-righteousness, but she remained acutely aware of many flaws and failures. "I am very far from practicing what I understand, and still the desire alone I have of doing it gives me peace," she said.

Among her many monastic slip-ups was her habit of dozing off during periods of corporate prayer and worship, but such failures did not induce guilt or lessen her love. "I am far from being a saint," she said, "[but] I am not desolate. I remember that little children are as pleasing to their parents when they are asleep as well as when they are wide awake."

Lessons from a "Little" One

Thérèse lived and died in the nineteenth century and was canonized in the twentieth century, but I believe she is a wonderful saint for the twenty-first century, because there are so many profound lessons she can teach those of us who struggle to express a simple faith in today's intensely competitive, high-tech, money-driven, bigger-is-better world.

One thing Thérèse shows us is that you don't need to be sinless or smart or sophisticated to be a mystic who is lovingly connected to Jesus. As one writer said, "Her ordinary existence was material for extraordinary holiness."

Thérèse also shows us what true commitment means. We invited a Thérèse scholar to lead a retreat at our community a few years ago. I remember her saying that Thérèse did not report having one spiritual consolation from God from the day she entered Carmel until her death nine years later. But she hung in there anyway.

This kind of commitment during a spiritually "dry" period speaks volumes to me, especially in the context of a feeling-oriented spirituality and a culture in which commitments seem to mean so little to so many. Many of us probably would have "discerned" that God did not really want us in any community where we were not continually showered with blessings and affirmation. But Thérèse remained faithful to her commitment (and if she hadn't, we would not know of the marvelous saint we honor and love today). This lesson about her commitment is monumental for me.

Thérèse's life also shows what an important calling parenting can be. I know that many parents worry about their children. They struggle to instill a sense of faith and love for God, hoping all the time that their efforts will prevail against a flood of negative, cynical messages driven home by a pervasive pop culture. But Thérèse's parents showed that with devotion and commitment, it is still possible to raise a saint.

And as the head of a community, I also appreciate the attitude Thérèse had toward others at Carmel. Instead of associating with the sisters she thought might bring her the most pleasure, she sought to be a good Samaritan to those who were the most annoying.

Today, most of us are very attuned to the rhetoric of abuse and victimization. And when it comes to being abused, most of us adapt the motto found on the old Texas flag: "Don't tread on me." But

Thérèse viewed her trials in the light of eternity, finding in them a means for turning the trials and tribulations of daily life into opportunities for exhibiting the loving grace of Christ.

"I am a little brush which Jesus has chosen in order to paint His own image in the souls you entrusted to my care," she said. And perhaps from studying her brief and humble life, we can all learn a little bit more about how we can be God's brushes, painting beautiful portraits of love, devotion, and service.

LEARNING MORE ABOUT
Thérèse of Lisieux

Story of a Soul: The Autobiography of St. Thérèse of Lisieux is a spiritual classic and is surely one of the most moving and accessible books by any of the mystics featured in this book. It is available in many translations and editions. We relied most heavily on John Clarke's translation (Institute of Carmelite Studies, 1975).

John Beevers's 1950 biography, *Storm of Glory: The Story of St. Thérèse of Lisieux* (Image) is still remarkably readable, but a newer biography by Kathryn Harrison—*St. Thérèse of Lisieux* (part of the Penguin Lives series published by Viking, 2003)—brings new research and sensibilities to bear on an amazing story.

Patrick Ahern's *Maurice & Thérèse: The Story of a Love* was the source of the information in this chapter's sidebar. The book presents an interesting perspective on a previously unknown aspect of Thérèse's one-to-one outreach to troubled souls (Doubleday, 1998; Image, 2001).

Testimony to Thérèse's continuing popularity can be found in *St. Thérèse in Ireland: Official Diary of the Irish Visit, April-July 2001*, published by Dublin-based Columba Press.

And in 2004, director Leonardo Defilippis unveiled a new film about the saint called *Thérèse*. The film should be available on video and DVD in 2005.

The Way of the Modern Mystic
Thomas Merton

The close circle of friends who drank, danced, and debated the finer points of literature, cinema, jazz, and politics with Thomas Merton in New York in the 1930s were shocked when the one-time atheist told them he would be entering the Catholic Church. They were flabbergasted when he announced that he wanted to become a priest—a decision he had made while recovering from the latest in a series of nasty hangovers. But by the time he decided to become a monk at a Trappist monastery in Kentucky, they had exhausted all their remaining reserves of wonder.

"We'll probably never hear from him again," said Mark Van Doren, one of Merton's professors at Columbia University, as his former student headed off to the monastic community of the Abbey of Gethsemani. "He's leaving the world."

As predictions go, this one was pretty far off the mark. For once Merton was established in the silence, solitude, and seclusion of Gethsemani, his inner mystic and his inner muse began working overtime to create a vast outpouring of books, including volumes of poetry, theology, history, comparative religion, contemplative spirituality, Christian social activism, autobiography, photography, and drawings that would rapidly make him the most famous and influential monk of the twentieth century.

He had a major influence on me at a time in my spiritual pilgrimage when I was beginning to consider both monasticism and Catholicism. I remember visiting the local library in Munster, Indiana, to find some books on Christian community. On the shelf next to titles about Anabaptist groups like the Amish and the Mennonites was Merton's *The Silent Life*—an overview of the "White Monk" reforms of the eleventh century and their impact on monastic communities today. I devoured it, and soon after that read two more of his books: *Seven Storey Mountain* and *The Sign of Jonas*. These led me to his work on contemplative prayer and spiritual direction, which were very helpful.

I continued reading Merton after my move to Alverna, the now-closed Franciscan retreat center in Indianapolis. I also made several trips to Gethsemani with one of the brothers from Alverna. And Merton's example as a monk, a mystic, a writer, and a seeker after truth continues to inspire me today, as I seek to follow Jesus within the Brothers and Sisters of Charity at Little Portion hermitage in Arkansas.

Merton wrote about so many things that it might be easier for us to list the subjects Merton *didn't* address than to try doing justice to the vast array of topics he subjected to his passionate and often piercing analysis. The Desert Fathers? Merton published a collection of their sayings and assessed their lasting impact in his book, *The Wisdom of the Desert*. Zen Buddhism? He explored that subject in two books: *Zen Masters* and *Zen and the Birds of Appetite*. Shaker aesthetics? Merton paid tribute to the utopian religious group's perspective on life and art in his own book, *Seeking Paradise: The Spirit of the Shakers*, and he contributed an essay on Shaker furniture to another author's project.

Merton died in 1968, and a compendium of his life and work can be found in *The Thomas Merton Encyclopedia*, published in 2002 (Orbis). But this encyclopedia is already out of date, as new books culled from Merton's vast journals and books written about him by scholars and members of the International Thomas Merton Society continue to fly off presses around the world. (Two interesting new additions to the growing Merton catalog include his own work, *Dialogues with Silence* (HarperSanFrancisco)—a gift book collecting some of his prayers, as well as one hundred of his Zen-like pen-and-ink drawings—and Henri J. Nouwen's *Encounters with Merton* (Crossroad/Carlisle).

Rather than attempt (and inevitably fail) to do justice to the many facets of this modern-day religious renaissance man, this brief chapter focuses more narrowly on Merton's vital inner life, and it is there that we will find the keys for unlocking some of the more astounding paradoxes of his unique life and lasting legacy.

How, for example, did a man who submitted to the Trappists' vow of silence come to write more words than many people will read in a lifetime? Or how did a man who entered into a life of religious seclusion become a committed Christian activist who spoke out on global issues of war, racism, and economic injustice? And how did a man who delved deeply into his own faith's mystical and monastic resources emerge as an ambassador to other faiths in the years before Vatican II declared such efforts an urgent necessity?

By seeing how this one man blazed a trail through these seeming contradictions, we can all learn something about how we can live vital spiritual lives that reflect both our love of God and our concern for the complex and often chaotic world in which we find ourselves.

A Man of Many Riches

Memoirs by monks don't typically rocket up the best-seller charts, but that's what happened with Merton's *The Seven Storey Mountain* after it arrived in bookstores in the fall of 1948. A candid account that began with his birth in France and continued through his first three years at Gethsemani, the book sold more than half a million copies in its first year and was soon translated into twenty foreign languages, establishing the thirty-three-year-old Merton's credentials as a passionate and literate Christian thinker.

Merton inherited his wanderlust and his love of art from his father and his sense of religious skepticism from his mother, who died of stomach cancer when he was six. Even though he had no formal religious training, he possessed an innate religious imagination. As he traveled across Europe with his father, he was repeatedly moved by the majesty of medieval church ruins, which he said forced you, "in spite of yourself, to be at least a virtual contemplative."

He wasn't sure what to make of Catholics or Protestants, but after studying at an English boarding school, he dismissed Anglicanism as "a class religion" whose members were held together by "the powerful attraction of their own social tradition."

Merton's father died when he was sixteen, and following a period of grief and depression came a sense of liberation. "I found myself completely stripped of everything that impeded the movement of my own will to do as it pleased," he wrote. "I imagined that I was free."

Freedom quickly led to nihilism, a flirtation with Communism, and the futile pursuit of sensual gratification. "The love of pleasure is destined by its very nature to defeat itself and end in frustration," he wrote, reflecting on a period of youthful experimentation fueled by drunken parties (one featuring a mock crucifixion) and brief romances that often led to sex and, in at least one important case, resulted in unwanted pregnancy.

This romance ended in a legal settlement that led to the loss of his scholarship at Cambridge, despair and thoughts of suicide, and his eventual move to the United States, where he enrolled at Columbia University, put his past behind him, and quickly became a Big Man on Campus.

Outwardly witty and garrulous, Merton was often the center of attention at parties where anyone within earshot became spellbound with his stories and jokes. But inwardly, he was experiencing a growing sense of sickness and sorrow over the emptiness and spiritual corruption of his life. He would later write about his mounting dissatisfaction:

> If what most people take for granted were really true—if all you
> needed to be happy was to grab everything and see everything and

investigate every happy experience and then talk about it, I should have been a very happy person, a spiritual millionaire.

His reading of Blake, Joyce, Waugh, Shakespeare, Hopkins, and Huxley repeatedly forced him to confront the big questions of life for which he had no sufficient answers. He was also reading Aquinas and John of the Cross, but books by Catholic writers fueled his religious ambivalence. "While I admired Catholic *culture*, I had always been afraid of the Catholic Church," he wrote.

During a trip to Cuba, Merton attended mass at a Catholic church where he had an encounter with God:

> God in all His essence, all His power, all His glory. . . . The unshakable certainty, the clear and immediate knowledge that heaven was right in front of me, struck me like a thunderbolt and went through me like a flash of lightning and seemed to lift me clean up off the earth.

He continued attending mass back in New York, but his prayers were interrupted by a voice spurring him on to greater commitment. "What are you waiting for?" it asked. "You know what you ought to do. Why don't you do it?"

The twenty-three-year-old Merton was accepted into the Catholic Church in 1938 and began seeking ways to live out his faith more fully. Soon he contemplated becoming a monk, finally settling on the Franciscan order. But his efforts were derailed by complications surrounding his having fathered a child. This setback was hard on him, and during confession with a priest, Merton burst into sobs over his many failings and his dashed hopes.

He had all but given up on the idea of being a monk by the time he went to Gethsemani for a retreat, but his experience there transformed him. "Here, suddenly, I am in the Court of the Queen of Heaven," he wrote in his journal.

Merton returned to Gethsemani for good near the end of 1941. "I want to give God everything," he told the abbot who admitted him

Thomas Merton and His Time

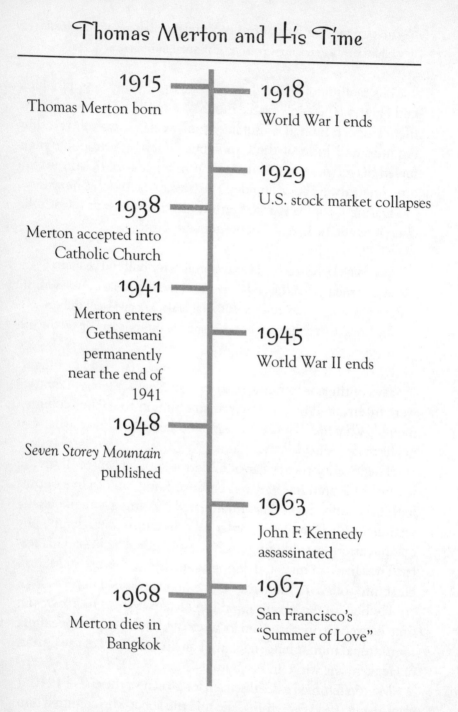

1915
Thomas Merton born

1918
World War I ends

1929
U.S. stock market collapses

1938
Merton accepted into
Catholic Church

1941
Merton enters
Gethsemani
permanently
near the end of
1941

1945
World War II ends

1948
Seven Storey Mountain
published

1963
John F. Kennedy
assassinated

1968
Merton dies in
Bangkok

1967
San Francisco's
"Summer of Love"

to the cloister. He was twenty-seven years old, and the monastery would be his home for the remaining twenty-seven years of his life.

A Thoroughly Modern Monk

"The monk in hiding himself from the world becomes not less himself, not less of a person, but more of a person, more truly and perfectly himself," wrote the newest resident of Gethsemani. But Merton's joy didn't mean things were easy in this community of Trappists, who are better known as the Order of Cistercians of the Strict Observance. "Life was arduous, confined, raw," wrote biographer Michael Mott.

The monks subsisted on meager diets for half the year, and they never ate meat, fish, or eggs. Winters were so cold that the holy water in the chapel froze, and Merton and the other monks routinely came down with colds. Labor was compulsory. Penance and prayer were solemn duties. Monks slept in their habits, which were washed once a month, and showers could be taken only with permission of the abbot. Old tin cans served as communal drinking cups. Other policies were even more challenging for the once sociable Merton: the monks kept complete silence, communicating among themselves by sign language only when necessary, and mail could only be sent to the outside world four times a year.

But Merton's soul blossomed in this harsh and silent environment. "The monastery is a school," he wrote, "a school in which we learn from God how to be happy."

We can be thankful that Gethsemani's abbot appreciated literature and encouraged Merton's writing. Poetry, theology, and autobiographical journals flowed from his pen. Some of these journal entries became the raw material for *The Seven Storey Mountain*, whose success stunned Merton and dramatically changed life at the once sleepy monastery. As the book's sales soared, Merton was the subject of magazine profiles in *The Atlantic* and *Life*, and he was the subject of a TV teleplay.

During the 1950s, Gethsemani was flooded with so much fan mail that it took a handful of monks to answer it all. Some of the letters were critical. "Tell this talking Trappist who took a vow of silence to *shut up!*" wrote one angry correspondent. But most of the mail was favorable. Some letters from female fans were so adoring that the mailroom monks thought them inappropriate.

They did their best to insulate their brother from the consequences of his growing fame, but he was still forced to deal with many requests himself. "I am bombarded by beggars, fakers, con-men, business men," he said. Meanwhile, his vow of poverty served to insulate him from the millions of dollars that flowed into the monastery during the course of his long and prolific literary career. He never saw a penny of his vast earnings.

While Merton the author was becoming an international celebrity, Merton the monk was seeking greater solitude and seclusion. He was granted the use of an old tool shed, which he converted into a daytime hermitage and where he drank deeply of the work of John of the Cross and other apophatic mystics. "We must always walk in darkness," he wrote. "We must travel in silence. We must fly by night."

Merton became a devoted student of the inner life. But ironically, the vitality of his own interior spirituality propelled him outward into the worlds of literature, comparative religion, international affairs, and social activism. He wrote:

> Any man may be called . . . to be fused into one spirit with Christ in the furnace of contemplation and then go forth and cast upon the earth that same fire which Christ wills to see enkindled. If this sublime fire of infused love burns in your soul, it will inevitably send forth throughout the Church and the world an influence more tremendous than could be estimated by the radius reached by words or by example.

A Compassionate Activist

The 1960s were a time of turmoil and transition. But while issues of war and peace, racism, women's rights, and social justice raged beyond the monastery walls, most monks were content to tune out the cacophony of the outside world and focus on their prayers and devotions. But not Merton, who had seen social inequalities first-hand while volunteering at Catherine de Hueck's Friendship House in Harlem during his years at Columbia. He even coined a phrase—"active contemplation"—that summarized his efforts to combine the quiet solitude of the cloister with the social conscience of the Christian activist.

The monks at Gethsemani were prohibited from seeing newspapers, but Merton found other ways to keep abreast of the world's problems. His reading of Latin American writers helped him understand the ways injustice, oppression, and violence conspired to punish the world's poorest citizens. His correspondence with Christian pacifists like Daniel Berrigan and John Howard Yoder deepened his opposition to war in general and the war in Viet Nam in particular. And as he listened to recordings by Bob Dylan and Joan Baez, he came to understand that these pop poets spoke for a growing youth counterculture that was fed up with organized religion but hungry for spiritual reality and committed to social justice.

Soon a tide of words was pouring from Merton's pen. There were articles like "Peace: A Religious Responsibility," "Passivism and Resistance," "Cold War Letters," and "Letters to a White Liberal." There were books such as *Breakthrough to Peace, Twelve Views on the Threat of Thermonuclear Extermination, Seeds of Destruction, Faith and Violence, Peace in the Post-Christian Era,* and *Gandhi on Non-Violence.* And there were such poems as "Chant to Be Used in Processions Around a Site with Furnaces"—his personal response to the horrors of the Holocaust.

Merton was not a pacifist. And he was an outspoken critic of the antiwar zealot "who 'loses himself' in his cause in such a way that he can no longer 'find himself' at all." Still, he favored nonviolent approaches to resolving disputes over military means. And as he researched twenty centuries worth of Christian approaches to war and peace, he found support for his views in the writings of Church Fathers like Tertullian and Origen. These and other saints of old seemed more concerned about the repercussions of violence than was Augustine, whose writings on "just war" theory have been called on to justify everything from the medieval crusades to America's 2003 invasion of Iraq.

The reaction to Merton's social writings came fast and furious. The Catholic press attacked many of his ideas, but he was unable to defend or clarify his positions because his superiors in the Trappist order censored much of his social justice writing and ultimately prohibited him from publishing anything on nonviolence. "I am to stop all publication on anything on war," he wrote in his journal. "Monk concerned with peace. Bad image."

But Merton felt so strongly about his views that he exploited a loophole in his restrictions, sending mimeographed copies of his writings to opinion leaders around the world. "I am perhaps at the turning point of my spiritual life," he wrote in his journal. "Walking into a known and definite battle. May God protect me in it."

On April 12, 1962, Merton received public recognition for his efforts when his "Prayer for Peace" was read in the U.S. House of Representatives and entered into the *Congressional Record*. The prayer succinctly captured his overriding concerns: "Grant us prudence in proportion to our power, Wisdom in proportion to our science, Humanness in proportion to our wealth and might."

Later that same year, Catholic leaders from around the world gathered in Rome for the opening sessions of the Second Vatican Council. Many of the documents coming out of Vatican II stressed the importance of social justice, and the papal encyclical *Pacem in Terris* (Peace on Earth) seemed like a ringing endorsement of many of Merton's ideas.

It finally seemed that the worldwide church was coming around to his point of view, but he neither gloated nor complained. "I am not sore, not even interested any more," he wrote. "I did what I thought ought to be done and that is that."

A Mystic for Our Times

The depth of Merton's mystical inner life fueled his tireless activities in the wider world, demonstrating that spiritual experience needn't render one impotent and silent. Merton's life also shows that ancient monastic traditions can still provide a wealth of resources to those who seek a deep and vibrant relationship with God in our own day.

Near the end of *The Seven Storey Mountain*, Merton describes "the peak of the mystical life" as "a marriage of the soul with God which gives the saints a miraculous power, a smooth and tireless energy in working for God and for souls, which bears fruit in the sanctity of thousands and changes the course of religious and secular history."

As we near the end of this book, it is fitting to consider the many ways Merton made monasticism attractive and accessible to so many people. Although most of us are not necessarily called to join a monastery, he demonstrates that the ancient monastic and mystical traditions still have much to teach all of us today.

First, these traditions remind us to live for God and God "alone." Jesus clearly taught that those who want to be his disciples must renounce everything in order to follow him. Or, as St. Evagrios put it, we must "renounce all to gain everything." What does this mean for us? In some cases, it means giving up our sense of entitlement to the things in our life in order that we might use them properly.

Do we selfishly try to possess the people we love, or do we first let them go in order to love them without possessiveness in the care of God? And closer to home, do we let go of our very self in order to find ourselves in the self-emptying divine love of Jesus? The monks and mystics of the past can teach us these valuable lessons in the present.

Second, Merton shows us that the monks of old can still provide us with a pattern for how we might carve out part of our hectic lives and create an environment that contributes to our life with God. The monks made their whole life a good environment for meditation and prayer. Do we use the tools given us by God to help make our whole life a beautiful prayer? Do we go to church to immerse ourselves in an environment of prayer through word, sacrament, and fellowship? Do we have a place for prayer in the home? Do we set aside daily time for meditation and prayer?

Many teachers believe that setting aside a mere twenty minutes of meditation time per day can help us along the road to deeper devotion. This tithing of our time for the practice of meditation, which sets the stage for the kinds of real contemplation that provides God the opportunity to enter our lives more deeply and radically, can transform us in ways that will affect us throughout the rest of the day. For some people, the morning is the best time for meditation; others prefer the evening. If you can't decide which is best, try both!

Merton's social consciousness is also important, for it shows in a powerful way that one can be a contemplative *and* a hermit—a monk *and* an activist who has a practical impact for world peace and justice. In my own life, Merton's example helped inspire my work with Mercy Corps—the international Catholic relief organization—as well as the founding of our monastic mission on the island of Ometepe in the Diocese of Granada, Nicaragua. Merton had hoped to establish a hermitage in Nicaragua, and now it seems our foundation fulfills a wish he never saw completed.

Finally, Merton and the many other monks and mystics of the past two thousand years teach us to find real and lasting unity with each other through the divestiture of self in Christ. Monks like Merton found that their spiritual disciplines helped them live in oneness and communion with their brothers and sisters in Christ, as well as the whole human family. What about you? Do you live in community with others, or are you a "lone-ranger Christian"? By finding ways to connect with others in community, you will deepen your experience of God's transforming love.

The monks and mystics of yesterday still have much to teach us today. May we learn the lessons of the ancients of the faith and apply it to our lives today in ways that make our whole lives into beautiful prayers to God.

"There is intoxication in the waters of contemplation," wrote Merton. And like so many saints from ages past, he is urging us to dive in and see for ourselves. Or, as he wrote in the Latin postscript to *The Seven Storey Mountain*, "Sit finis libri, non finis quaerendi." Translated into English, the postscript reads: "Let this be the ending of the book but by no means the end of the searching."

Bridging East and West

Thomas Merton was a devoted student of Christian mysticism, and he scoured the writings of both Eastern Christian monks and Russian Orthodox mystics, adopting much of what he learned into his own spiritual practice, including the Hesychast Jesus Prayer (see the chapter entitled "The Way of the Pilgrim").

As he reflected on the insights he had gained from Eastern Christians, he decided to work toward building bridges between the long-separated Eastern and Western branches of the Christian family:

> If I can unite in myself, in my own spiritual life, the thought of the East and the West, of the Greek and Latin Fathers, I will have created in myself a reunion of the divided Church and from that unity in myself can come the exterior and visible unity of the Church. For if we want to bring together East and West we cannot do it by imposing one upon the other. We must contain both in ourselves, and transcend both in Christ.

Merton also studied the works of Buddhist and Hindu thinkers, and he developed relationships with internationally acclaimed Zen teacher Daisetsu Suzuki, Buddhist monk Thich Nhat Hanh, and exiled Tibetan Buddhist leader the Dalai Lama. Merton saw a vitality in Eastern monasticism that he perceived as lacking in Western monasticism, which he judged to be in a state of crisis.

He was not a universalist, if by *universalism* one means the belief that all religions are equally valid and equally redemptive. In fact, he railed against "Baptizing Buddhism" and criticized those ecumenicists who he felt engaged in "spurious attempts to bring East and West together" in "laughable syncretisms."

But he was a universalist in the sense that he believed the gospel of Christ was for everyone. "My Catholicism is all the world and all ages," he wrote. "It dates from the beginning of the world."

In 1968, Merton was invited to participate in a conference hosted by Benedictine and Cistercian monks in Thailand. He

(continued)

Bridging East and West (continued)

gratefully accepted the invitation, in part because it would give him a chance to visit a region of the world that he had read about for decades.

"I go with an open mind," he wrote. "My hope is simply to enjoy the long journey, profit by it, learn, change, and perhaps find something or someone who will help me advance in my own spiritual quest."

He also added this prophetic comment: "Whether or not I will end my days here, I don't know—and perhaps it is not so important. The great thing is to respond perfectly to God's will in this providential opportunity, whatever it may bring."

Included on his Asian itinerary was a speech to a group of Chinese Christian nuns about the need for East-West dialogue. "We need the religious genius of Asia and Asian culture to inject a dimension of depth into our aimless threshing about," he said. "These are some of the things we must recover and you are going to help us do it."

By the time Merton arrived at the site of the Thailand conference, he was both exhilarated and exhausted. After giving a morning lecture on Marxism and monasticism, he joined others for lunch, then retired to his room for a rest. He died that afternoon when a malfunctioning fan electrocuted him. The telegram announcing his death crossed the international dateline to arrive at Gethsemani on December 10, 1968—the twenty-seventh anniversary of the day Merton entered the monastery.

LEARNING MORE ABOUT

Thomas Merton

As I soon discovered after I read my first Merton book, he wrote dozens more volumes, covering an unbelievably wide range of topics and making him an unusually varied and complex Christian mystic and thinker.

His legacy survived him, as did the words he had given earlier at an interfaith conference in India. "The deepest level of communication is not communication, but communion," he said. "It is wordless. It is beyond words, and it is beyond speech, and it is beyond concept."

Having followed Merton's work, I was intrigued by his interfaith adventures, but like others who came from a more theologically conservative evangelical background, I initially struggled with feelings that he had wandered too far afield from the core of the Christian faith. I even wondered if God had cut his life short in the midst of his Asian trip so that he would not be able to mislead other fellow believers.

Over time, I have come to a deeper appreciation of the wisdom and balance he exhibited in this final phase of his life. I can understand his sense of awe and respect for Buddhism and have tried to find appropriate ways to integrate aspects of that into my own Christian experience without compromising my Christian faith in any way. I now believe that a healthy appreciation of other religions has added to the depth of my own faith and has ultimately made me a better follower of Jesus and a more faithful son of the church. I learned much of this from Merton.

Thomas Merton was a complex man who applied the riches of his Christian faith to many areas of life. But at his most basic he was a mystic, and his mysticism connected him not only to the heart of his own faith but to the faith of other believers around the world.

Two of the best books are among the biggest. His 460-page autobiography, *The Seven Storey Mountain*, remains a powerful book more than half a century after it was first published. In 1998, Harcourt Brace released a fiftieth-anniversary edition of this classic, featuring helpful introductory essays by Merton's original editor and the founding president of the International Thomas Merton Society.

Michael Mott's critically acclaimed biography, *The Seven Mountains of Thomas Merton* (Houghton Mifflin, 1984), is nearly six hundred pages long (not including another hundred pages of end matter); in addition to being thorough, it is surprisingly accessible.

From there, the student of Merton can go in any number of directions. *No Man Is an Island* (its title is an allusion to the work of John Donne) and *Thoughts in Solitude* feature contemplative writing. *The Wisdom of the Desert* is a concise look at the Desert Fathers and their continuing relevance today. *The Waters of Siloe* is an interesting history of the Cistercian Order. Among the most recent books, *Dialogues with Silence: Complete Prayers and Selected Drawings* (HarperSanFrancisco, 2003) is well worthwhile.

If you're interested in Merton but aren't sure where to start, check out the Web site of the International Thomas Merton Society (www.merton.org), which features a detailed bibliography of his works, a thorough chronology of his life, and updates on activities by Merton scholars worldwide. Or skim through *The Thomas Merton Encyclopedia* (Orbis, 2002), which won the "Best Reference Work" award at the 2003 Annual Convention of the Catholic Press Association. Merton probably wrote a number of books on topics that might interest you, and these sources can help you find the titles you're looking for.

Some of my songs that were inspired by Merton can be found on the album *Meditations from Solitude*.

The Authors

John Michael Talbot is the author of nearly twenty books and is a best-selling Christian musician whose forty-seven albums have sold more than four million copies. His liturgical, meditative sacred music and contemporary compositions are sung in Protestant and Catholic churches around the world.

John and his brother Terry were members of the pioneering country-rock band Mason Proffit, which performed with the Grateful Dead, Jefferson Airplane, and Janis Joplin. After a mystical encounter with Christ transformed his life, Talbot left the trappings of the secular music world to play a pioneering role in the Contemporary Christian Music (CCM) movement, as he began to create best-selling Christian recordings as a solo artist. After his conversion to Catholicism, he founded The Brothers and Sisters of Charity, an integrated monastic community with forty members residing at its Motherhouse in Arkansas; the community operates a mission in Nicaragua and has more than five hundred members worldwide who live in their own homes.

Through his books, his recordings, and his live performances, Talbot reaches tens of thousands of people every year. He is sought-after as a teacher and lecturer on the subjects of simple and monastic living, St. Francis of Assisi, Christian meditation, and music ministry. He has also been the subject of major media coverage by *People* magazine, the *Wall Street Journal*, ABC's "Good Morning America," *Our Sunday Visitor*, *Christianity Today*, *Billboard*, and *The Hollywood Reporter*.

Steve Rabey is a freelance writer who has authored or coauthored nearly twenty books, including *Rachel's Tears*, which was a *Publishers Weekly* Religion and Christian Booksellers Association bestseller, and the acclaimed book on Celtic spirituality, *In the House of Memory*.

He has written nearly two thousand articles about religion, spirituality, history, and popular culture for magazines, newspapers, and Web sites. His work has appeared in the *New York Times*, the *Los Angeles Times*, the *Washington Post*, *Christianity Today*, *Catholic Digest*, *New Age*, and *Publishers Weekly*. Rabey previously collaborated with Talbot on *The Music of Creation* (Jeremy Tarcher, 1999) and the acclaimed *The Lessons of St. Francis: Simplicity and Spirituality in Your Daily Life* (Dutton/Plume, 1997/1998). He lives in Colorado with his wife, Lois, an author and speaker.